L. R. KLEIN
AN ESSAY ON THE THEORY OF
ECONOMIC PREDICTION

L. R. KLEIN

An Essay on the Theory of Economic Prediction

MARKHAM PUBLISHING COMPANY
CHICAGO

MARKHAM ECONOMICS SERIES
JULIUS MARGOLIS, EDITOR

ARROW, *Theory of Risk Bearing*

BOWLES and KENDRICK, *Notes and Problems in Microeconomic Theory: A Program Learning Approach with Solutions*

BUCHANAN, *Cost and Choice; An Inquiry in Economic Theory*

HAVEMAN and MARGOLIS, *Public Expenditures and Policy Analysis*

KLEIN, *An Essay on the Theory of Economic Prediction*

PREFACE TO ORIGINAL EDITION

It was a great privilege and pleasure to be able to deliver the Yrjö Jahnsson lectures in 1968 (April 1—5, 1968) at the University of Helsinki. The material and thoughts on the subject of economic prediction were outgrowths of econometric research done at the University of Pennsylvania during the past decade. The opportunity to put these thoughts to paper came during a leave of absence from my home University while I held the Ford Visiting Research Professorship at the University of California (Berkeley). I am grateful to that fine institution, known as the Berkeley-Stanford Seminar on Mathematical Economics, for an opportunity to have a preliminary airing of my views on prediction.

Further ideas that were stimulated during the course of my visit to Helsinki enabled me to amend the presentation and put some final touches on theoretical issues. I am grateful to the Yrjö Jahnsson Foundation for the invitation to come to Finland and for the opportunity to place my ideas on prediction before Finnish academicians.

August, 1968, Philadelphia, Pa., USA

Lawrence R. Klein

PREFACE TO THE AMERICAN EDITION

In order to make the material from the Yrjö Jahnsson lectures more easily available for readers in the Western Hemisphere, I have prepared this American edition.

The awkwardness of transatlantic communications was responsible for a few minor typographical errors in the original edition. These have been corrected, and some notes have been added to update tables and references.

In the original lectures there was inadequate time to go through the details of the actual forecasting procedures that have been developed during the past few years in the Wharton Econometric Forecasting Unit. In an appendix containing entirely new material, the forecast of summer 1969 is fully explained. Since a forecast from a large model involves the production of massive tables, the data have been condensed to a summary form consistent with the purposes of this volume.

The occasion of the Yrjö Jahnsson Lectures motivated an investigation on my part of estimation procedures for predictive efficiency. Some of the early results, still fragmentary, are explained in a final part of the new appendix material. These are direct applications and tests of the estimation methods discussed in the *Essay*.

Lawrence R. Klein

April 1970, Philadelphia, Pa.

CONTENTS

An Essay on the Theory of
Economic Prediction

Many gifted individuals have successfully made important predictions about the future course of economic life. In some cases their remarkable insights have been demonstrated on singular occasions, but in a few cases individuals have consistently made accurate predictions over and over again. Unfortunately, the accomplishments at foresight of the gifted individuals have not been passed on to future generations in the form of systematic techniques that could be assimilated and applied by others. Until recently economic prediction has been artistic, subjective, and personal. It is my belief that we have made progress in modern quantitative economics towards developing a scientific approach to economic prediction that can now be given some rudiments of theory in a form that will enable pupils of today's forecasters to apply the same methods and achieve comparable degrees of precision. I shall concentrate, in this essay, on the use of the *objective* methods of econometrics as a systematic body of knowledge that can be passed on to future generations. The reader will soon find that this theory is not purely mechanical, devoid of judgment, or entirely reliant on statistical information, but it is a step in the direction towards scientific prediction and is as objective as possible.

9

FORMULATION OF THE PROBLEM

A great deal of, but not all, work in econometrics is concerned with the establishment of economic relationships, i.e. the familiar structural equations of the system such as demand functions, supply functions, production functions, price determination equations, and the like. These relationships are determined from sample data in such a way that a »close fit» is obtained between a parametric specification of the relationship and observations. In a general sense, this is a problem of *interpolation* with the sample boundaries. The principal problem of prediction is one of *extrapolation* beyond the confines of the sample.

The objective of statistical inference in the estimation of economic relationships is to obtain valid empirical generalizations about economic behavior. The objective in prediction is to be able to make generalizations to non sample situations. We usually associate the term »prediction» with an attempt to say what the future will actually be like, but viewed in the more general sense in which I am using the term in these lectures it encompasses a much wider range of ideas. I shall use the term »prediction» to mean the attempt to make scientific statements about non sample situations on the basis of relationships determined from sample observations. In this wider sense, I include attempts to say what the future will actually be as a special case of prediction but by no means the central aspect of the subject.

My attention will be focussed on economic prediction although many of the ideas could be extended to general social prediction. In some of the social sciences, there is little difference between their problems of statistical inference or prediction and those of economics, but in others the difficulties of measurement and quantification are so great that the techniques of prediction are not the same. To give some examples, statistical inference in demography and population projections seem to be hardly different in character from analogous methods in econometrics. More general sociological predictions or political predictions usually involve variables that we have not yet learned to measure or whose measurement may be inherently intractable, and formal methods of prediction like those of econometrics ought not to be contemplated at this time. An exception is voting behavior, and electoral prediction may involve essentially the same problems as economic prediction. Indeed electoral prediction and demographic prediction may be greatly improved by proper blending with economic prediction. Well known cases of failures can be cited to indicate that sound economic prediction would have improved electoral and demographic prediction, but the argument works both ways.[1] Economic prediction can be aided by good sociological and political prediction. The whole process of social behavior is involved in prediction in most of the fields of social science. Ultimately, the issue is to construct good social models that can be applied to prediction in many areas simultaneously. From the point of view of econometric type methodology, I shall not try to deal in full with non quantifiable subjects, and to keep the presentation within bounds of familiar material, I shall concentrate on economic prediction, with due allowance for the *exogenous* effect of other social science variables.

There is one further limitation that I would like to make in a specific way. The approach will be non clinical. I shall not take up the question of predicting Mr. A's or Company X's economic behavior; I shall be interested only in predicting Mr.

1. Specific instances are the U.S. presidential elections of 1960 (recession period) and U.S. population projections made during the Great Depression.

Average Man's or The Economy's performance. In some social sciences, clinical methods can be used and judgments made about individual behavior. I might want to make use of sample data about individuals, but I do not want to make predictions about individuals as such. This is not the same thing as the distinction between micro and macro econometrics; it is a distinction between a personal and an impersonal interest.

WHY PREDICT?

Prediction is obviously interesting in its own right. It is an interesting intellectual challenge to see if prediction is possible. Economics and econometric method can claim scientific status if they enable the professional worker to do better than the layman with extraordinary intuition and »feel» for the economy. Then the balance between science and art in forecasting can be shifted towards the former.

It is frequently claimed that there is difference in methodology between making statistical inference about economic structure and predicting. I shall argue that they are part of one larger econometric problem and that prediction is a device that serves to test hypotheses about economic structure or improve estimates of economic structure. In predictive testing, we find deficiencies in estimated economic structure; this in turn gives us a basis for revising hypotheses and estimates. At the extreme, I shall propose a continuous testing procedure through the use of predictive criteria as a means of up dating and revising structural models; therefore I shall draw no distinction among structural estimation, theory testing, and prediction. They are all parts of one large problem.

12

TYPES OF PREDICTION

The standard form of prediction is an attempt to say what the future will be like. This, I shall call *ex ante prediction*. Before an event unfolds, we assemble as much pertinent information as possible — data already in existence — and extrapolate into the unknown. This is pure prediction.

In the wider sense of the term, as I am using it, we may use data already in existence to predict other data already in existence. If the latter data were not used in the sample from which the structure was estimated, we still have a prediction problem, but since the data to be predicted are already known, we term this *ex post prediction*. Such prediction can be either ahead (in time) of the sample or behind the sample. We might call *ex post prediction* ahead forecasting, in contrast with *ex post prediction* behind, which we might call backcasting.[1]

Prediction can be formulated as an unqualified statement about the future, regardless of external or exogenous events. This is called *unconditional prediction*, while a prediction that is qualified by assuming that some exogenous events must simultaneously occur is called *conditional prediction*. In the context of economic theory and analysis, *conditional prediction* is much more important and more widely used than is *unconditional prediction*. In commercial life, unconditional prediction has been predominant, but business planning might well make more use of conditional prediction.

Nearly all econometric work is based on statistical samples, and inferences are made under the guidance of the probability

1. See Martin Bronfenbrenner, »The Consumption Function Controversy», *Southern Economic Journal*, 14 (January, 1948), 304—20.

calculus. We often make econometric predictions as though we have a deterministic system, although this is hardly the case. Prediction from deterministic systems is called *non-stochastic prediction* to distinguish it from stochastic prediction, where we fully recognize the influence of random error on our judgements.

THE PREDICTION MODEL

The standard linear model of an economy can be written as

$$\sum_{i=o}^{p} A_i\, y_{t-i} + Bx_t = e_t.$$

A_o is an $n \times n$ nonsingular matrix of constant coefficients of dependent variables with typical element a_{ijo}.

A_i $(i = 1, 2, \ldots p)$ are $n \times n$ matrices of constant coefficients of lag variables, with maximum lag fixed at $i = p$. The typical element of A_k is a_{ijk}. All lags need not be present in each equation; therefore many elements of A_i are zero. Also, restrictions on the system may produce zero elements in A_o.

B is a rectangular matrix $(n \times m)$ of constant coefficients of independent variables, with typical element β_{ij}.

The dependent variables of the system, sometimes called endogenous variables, are

$$y_{t-i} = \left[(y_{1,\, t-i},\, y_{2,\, t-i},\, \ldots,\, y_{n,\, t-i}) \right]'.$$

The independent variables of the system, sometimes called exogenous variables, are

$$x_t = \left[(x_{1t},\, x_{2t},\, \ldots,\, x_{mt}) \right]'.$$

14

Lagged independent variables can simply be defined as new independent variables; therefore there is no reason to deal with such lags explicitly. The random error vector is

$$e_t = [(e_{1t}, e_{2t}, \ldots, e_{nt})]'.$$

The typical equation of this linear system is

$$\sum_{j=1}^{n} \sum_{k=0}^{p} a_{ijk} y_{j, t-k} + \sum_{j=1}^{m} \beta_{ij} x_{jt} = e_{it}, \qquad i = 1, 2, \ldots, n.$$

The model is written in *structural* form above. Corresponding to the structural form, we have a *reduced* form

$$y_t = A_o^{-1} \left(-\sum_{i=1}^{p} A_i y_{t-i} - B x_t + e_t \right) =$$

$$-A_o^{-1} \sum_{i=1}^{!p} A_i y_{t-i} - A_o^{-1} B x_t + A_o^{-1} e_t.$$

This is a convenient form from which to make predictions.

The typical equation is

$$y_{it} = \sum_{j=1}^{n} \sum_{k=1}^{p} \pi_{ijk} y_{j, t-k} + \sum_{j=1}^{m} \omega_{ij} x_{jt} + v_t \qquad i = 1, 2, \ldots, n.$$

The coefficients in this typical equation are functions of the structural coefficients a_{ijk} and β_{ij}. The random errors are linear functions of the errors in the structural equation.

The *final form* of a linear dynamic model is an equation system in which each dependent variable is expressed in terms of its

15

own lag values, independent variables (current and lagged), and random errors (current and lagged). We derive the *final form* as follows:[1] Let $A(L)$ be a polynomial expression in the lag operator

$$L^{\tau} y_t = y_{t-r} \qquad\qquad r = 0, 1, 2, \ldots, p$$

$$A(L) = A_o + A_1 L + A_2 L^2 + \ldots + A_p L^p$$

We may then write the dynamic system as

$$A(L) y_t = -B x_t + e_t$$

Let $a(L)$ denote the adjoint of $A(L)$ and $\varDelta(L) = |A(L)|$ denote the determinantal polynomial of $A(L)$. Premultiply both sides of the above equation by $a(L)$, and the resulting *final form* is

$$\| \varDelta(L) \| y_t = -a(L) B x_t + a(L) e_t,$$

where $\| \varDelta(L) \|$ is a matrix with $\varDelta(L)$ on the main diagonal and zeros everywhere else.

Each equation of the final form has identical autoregressive structure; i.e. it is a form in which each element of y is expressed as a function of its own lag structure (up to order np) and a lag function of independent variables and errors. The left hand sides are identical for each variable, while the right hand sides vary. In contrast with the *reduced form*, the final form induces

---

1. This presentation follows that in E. P. Howrey, »Dynamic Properties of Stochastic Linear Econometric Models». Econometric Research Program, memorandum No. 87, Princeton University, June, 1967, (unpublished).

an autoregressive error structure.[1] A typical equation of the final form is

$$\sum_{j=o}^{np} a_{ij} y_{i,\,t-j} = \sum_{j=1}^{m} \sum_{k=1}^{(n-1)p} b_{ijk} x_{j,\,t-k} + \sum_{j=1}^{n} \sum_{k=1}^{(n-1)p} c_{ijk} e_{j,\,t-k},$$

$$i = 1, 2, \ldots, n.$$

Finally, we come to the *solution* of the system. This is the summation of the system of finite difference equations. It could be derived from the original system directly, or more simply from each single equation in *final form*. The complete solution consists of the general solution of the homogeneous equation and a particular solution. From the *final form*, we may write the particular solution as

$$y_t = -\frac{a(L)}{\varDelta(L)} B x_t + \frac{a(L)}{\varDelta(L)} e_t.$$

The complete solution is

$$y_t = K\lambda^t - \frac{a(L)}{\varDelta(L)} B x_t + \frac{a(L)}{\varDelta(L)} e_t.$$

K is a matrix $(n \times np)$ of constants determined by the initial conditions of the system and λ is an np-element vector of roots of the characteristic polynomial associated with the autoregressive structure. This form of the system is convenient

1. These peculiar aspects of the final form have been noted at an early stage by L. Hurwicz, »Stochastic Models of Economic Fluctuations», *Econometrica* 12 (April, 1944), 114—24, and G. H. Orcutt, »A Study of the Autoregressive Nature of the Time Series Used for Tinbergen's Model of the Economic System of the United States, 1919—1932», *Journal of the Royal Statistical Society*, X (1948) Ser. B., 1—53.

for making predictions ahead for several periods (dynamic simulation). This form might be used either directly for prediction, or it may be used to show the implications of recursive solution of reduced form equations for several successive periods. It shows the distinctive roles of (1) internal dynamics from the elements of λ, (2) the time paths of independent variables, (3) the stochastic error accumulation.

There are significant differences among these ways of expressing a given set of linear equations. The structural coefficients have meaning and direct interpretation in terms of familiar economic concepts. They are the marginal propensities, elasticities, marginal productivities, reaction coefficients and other well understood parameters of the economy. They are grounded in received theory.

The reduced forms are used in estimation theory. They bridge the gap between the first and second stages of two-stage-least-squares. In prediction theory, they are multiplier equations, for short-run or impact multipliers. They also form the basis for single-period predictions.

The final forms show the dynamic or autoregressive structure of the system. They are convenient forms for obtaining solutions. In the final forms and solutions of the system, both error terms and independent variables are transformed. The lag transformations of error with rational function distributions $a(L)/\Delta(L)$ are important in showing the significance of the ideas of Frisch and Slutsky on the contribution of error accumulation to the explanation of cyclic phenomena.[1] They show

1. R. Frisch, »Propagation Problems and Impulse Problems in Dynamic Economics», Economic Essays in Honour of Gustav Cassel, 1933. E. Slutsky, »The Summation of Random Causes as the Source of Cyclic Processes», Econometrica 5 (April, 1937), 105—46.

that moving average processes of random series can produce cyclical series. The solution form of a linear dynamic economic system provides a rationale for expecting the random errors to be subjected to moving average processes.

The different types of prediction can be readily illustrated with reference to this explicit linear model. Consider the reduced form

$$y_t = -A_o^{-1} \sum_{i=1}^{p} A_i y_{t-i} - A_o^{-1} B x_t + A_o^{-1} e_t$$

In one-period ex-ante prediction, we attempt to forecast the values of y_t in future period $T+1$ at present time period T. The ex-ante forecast value, assuming estimated coefficients in A_i and B, is

$$y_{T+1}^f = -A_o^{-1} \sum_{i=1}^{p} A_i y_{T+1-i} - A_o^{-1} B x_{T+1}$$

We use known or estimated values of $y_T, y_{T-1}, + \cdots + y_{T-p+1}$ and x_{T+1} on the right hand side to evaluate y_{T+1} on the left. If $t = T, T-1, \ldots, T-p+1$ have already occurred but $T+1$ has not, we have an ex-ante situation. After having obtained ex-ante predictions y_{T+1}, we may continue to evaluate multi-period predictions by forming

$$y_{T+2}^f = -A_o^{-1} \sum_{i=1}^{p} A_i y_{T+2-i} - A_o^{-1} B x_{T+2},$$

where y_{T+1} is obtained from the previous prediction and the other lag values on the right hand side are known from the initial conditions. In a similar way we obtain y_{T+3}^f from ex-ante predictions of y_{T+2}, y_{T+1}, initial conditions, and assumed values of x_{T+3}, etc.

19

In an alternative approach, predictions ahead could be made from the solution equations

$$y_t = K\lambda^t - \frac{a(L)}{\Delta(L)} \, B \, x_t,$$

but these are better for showing the implications of forward projection than for actually carrying out the calculations.

If $t = T + 1$ were not a future period but had already occurred, and if the sample data that were used to estimate A_i, B did not include values for $t = T + 1$, we would call

$$y_{T+1}^f = -A_o^{-1} \sum_{i=1}^{p} A_i y_{T+1-i} - A_o^{-1} B \, x_{T+1}$$

an ex-post prediction. The difference between the ex-post and the ex-ante prediction lies in the facts that actual, not expected, values of x_{T+1} can be used and that the values of y_T, y_{T-1}, y_{T-p+1} are known more precisely. In multi-period ex-post predicting we can use either predicted values of the most recent lagged variables (y_{T+1}^f for obtaining y_{T+2}^f; y_{T+1}^f, y_{T+2}^f for obtaining y_{T+3}^f; etc.) or the actual values of the corresponding lagged variables. In addition, it is possible to verify immediately the accuracy of ex-post forecasts.

Both the ex-ante and the ex-post forecasts explicitly presented above are non-stochastic. We have assumed that

$$E(e_{T+1}) = E(e_{T+2}) = \ldots = 0,$$

and have substituted these expected values for e_{T+1}, e_{T+2}, etc. In stochastic prediction, we shall not know which values of e_{T+1}, e_{T+2}, etc. to use, but we can draw them from an estimated probability distribution and either present a range of predic-

20

tions based on alternative drawings with values of e_{T+1}, e_{T+2}, etc. added to the equation system for solution or present a long series of forward predictions with a single given set of random drawings. This would be stochastic prediction.[1]

If the values of x_{T+1}, x_{T+2}, etc. in the ex-ante prediction formulas for y_{T+1}, y_{T+2}, etc. are known with certainty or are *assumed* to be known without reservation, we have an unconditional ex-ante prediction (stochastic or non-stochastic). If there is uncertainty about the appropriate values of x_{T+1}, x_{T+2}, etc. we make predictions on the *condition* that certain values hold. We might write this as

$$y_{T+1}^f = -A_o^{-1} \sum_{i=1}^{p} A_i y_{T+1-i} - A_o^{-1} B x_{T+1}^c$$

to show that the prediction of y_{T+1} is conditional upon the value x_{T+1}^c holding. A range of predictions can be made for q different conditional values $x_{T+1}^{c_1}$, $x_{T+1}^{c_2}$, . . ., $x_{T+1}^{c_q}$.

We have not yet taken up the question of our knowledge of A_o, A_1, . . . A_p, B. These are not true parameter values in prediction formulas; they are numerical *estimates* of the true values. Conditions of structural change may be placed on these estimated parameter values for a prediction period. In this sense, too, we may have conditional predictions.

The formulation of the prediction problem is not essentially different if the basic model is not linear, but much of the reasoning is then implicit and not explicit; moreover the problems of error accumulation are then more complicated. I shall take the basic position that it is logically impossible to have a

---

1. Compare the results below on the construction of prediction intervals from the standard error of forecast.

completely linear economy.* The linear model has proved to be useful as a point of departure in econometric analysis, but it is highly unrealistic. In careful macroeconometric model studies nonlinear systems are usually developed, and it is worthwhile to give a formal statement of the prediction model in nonlinear terms.

The general nonlinear model is written as

$$f_i\left(y_{1t}, \cdots, y_{nt}, y_{1,\,t-1}, \cdots, y_{n,\,t-p}, x_{1t}, \cdots, x_{mt}\right) = e_{it}$$

$$i = 1, 2, \cdots, n.$$

The nonlinear functions depend on a set of parameters (not specified here) which may be estimated by nonlinear methods.

In some cases it may be possible to derive a closed-form expression

$$y_{it} = F_i(y_{1,\,t-1}, \cdots, y_{n,\,t-1}, \cdots, y_{n,\,t-p}, x_{1t}, \cdots, x_{mt}, e_{1t}, \cdots, e_{nt}).$$

There is no assurance, as in the linear case, that the error in such reduced form equations will be additive. In this sense we lose much of the advantage of the reduced form expression — separation of the predetermined parts and current stochastic parts of each dependent variable. Our customary approach is, therefore, different in the case of nonlinear systems. Having an estimate of parameters in such a system, we write it in the form

$$y_{it} = g_i(y_{1t}, \cdots, y_{nt}, y_{1,\,t-1}, \cdots, y_{n,\,t-p}, x_{1t}, \cdots, x_{mt}) + u_{it}$$

This is nearly always possible, given the kinds of nonlinearities that occur in econometric systems. Instead of developing *reduced forms, final forms* or explicit solution equations, we make numerical approximations to the solution of nonlinear equation

22

systems. A variety of solution algorithms can be used, but the method that now seems to be most appropriate is to obtain the non-stochastic solution from the iterative system[1]

$$y_{it}^{(r)} = g_i(y_{1t}^{(r)}, \cdots, y_{i-1,t}^{(r)}, y_{it}^{(r-1)}, \cdots, y_{nt}^{(r-1)} y_{1,t-1}, \cdots, y_{n,t-p},$$

$$x_{1t}, \cdots x_{mt})$$

$$\left| \frac{y_{it}^{(r)} - y_{it}^{(r-1)}}{y_{it}^{(r-1)}} \right| < \varepsilon \qquad\qquad i = 1, 2, \ldots, n.$$

Given initial approxminations, we iterate according to the previous equations until the set of dependent variables all change in absolute percentage terms by less than ε. We call the set of such values of y_{it} a solution for period t, given lagged values and values for x_{it}. The numerical solution serves as an alternative to the reduced form.

By using the solution values for period t as lagged input in period $t + 1$ together with lags from earlier periods and values of $x_{i, t+1}$ we can develop a similar numerical solution for $t + 1$. This procedure can be followed indefinitely for many periods. In this way we compute a dynamic solution to the non-stochastic linear system. This method has been used at some length to predict and obtain solutions from a large number of different models. It is extremely fast and efficient.[2]

Numerical stochastic solutions can be derived by adding random numbers to each equation in each solution period. In

1. This is commonly known as the Gauss—Seidel method of solving nonlinear simultaneous equation systems.

2. See the chapter by G. Fromm and L. R. Klein in the second volume of the Brookings Econometric Model Project, *The Brookings Model; Some Further Results* (Chicago: Rand McNally, 1969).

long period solutions, these errors do not accumulate additively, as in the linear case, but in the models studied so far the mean stochastic solutions have not differed appreciably from the non-stochastic solutions.[1]

PREDICTION ERROR

This subject will be studied from two points of view: 1. What is the theoretical range of ϵ ːor to be expected in prediction? 2. How should predictions be compared with reality and judged as satisfactory or unsatisfactory?

In a single prediction equation, the standard error of forecast is a well defined concept. The simplest case to consider is well-known but instructive to review as a point of departure. Given the »true linear relationship» in a reduced form

$$y_t = \sum_{i=1}^{m} \beta_i x_{it} + e_t,$$

the prediction

$$y_{T+1}^f = \sum_{i=1}^{m} \hat{\beta}_i x_{i,\,T+1}$$

is a random variable since it is based on sample estimates of the true coefficients β_i, and it replaces the unknown random error e_{T+1} by its expected value

$$Ee_t = 0.$$

1. See the chapter by A. L. Nagar, *ibid.*

The formula for standard error of forecast is

$$S^2_{y_{T+1}^f} = \sum_{i,j} S_{ij}\, x_{i,\,T+1}\, x_{j,\,T+1} + S^2_e,$$

where

S_{ij} = estimated covariance between $\hat{\beta}_i$ and $\hat{\beta}_j$

S^2_e = estimated variance of e_t.

If the estimation equation, which is already in reduced form, is also regarded as a structural equation and estimated as a least squares regression, we then have direct estimates of S_{ij} from

$$S_{ij} = S^2_e \left(\sum_{t=1}^{T} x_{it}\, x_{jt} \right)^{-1}$$

and estimates of S^2_e from

$$S^2_e = \frac{1}{T-m} \sum_{t=1}^{T} \left(y_t - \sum_{i=1}^{m} \hat{\beta}_i\, x_{it} \right)^2.$$

If the reduced form equation is derived from the inversion of a structural system, we must estimate S_{ij} (approximately) from the covariance estimates of the structural parameters. The statistic S^2_e is estimated as the residual variance (corrected appropriately for degrees of freedom) of the reduced form equation.

Forecast error as measured by $S^2_{y_{T+1}}$ is made up of two components. 1. There is imperfect knowledge of the true parameters β_i, and we use statistical estimates $\hat{\beta}_i$. The error contribution from the use of $\hat{\beta}_i$ is measured by S_{ij}, with weighting

25

by the magnitude of the associated exogenous variables $x_{i, T+1}$ $x_{j, T+1}$. The weight factors are variable; therefore the error variance depends on the magnitude of the exogenous variables at the time of prediction. If we were to transform the expression to measure variables in terms of deviations from the sample mean, we would have, instead, terms like

$$S_{ij} \left(x_{i, T+1} - \bar{x}_i \right) \left(x_{j, T+1} - \bar{x}_j \right).$$

This would indicate that larger error attaches to estimates made farther away from sample averages, in either direction, since S_{ij} is an element of a positive definite matrix and that smaller error attaches to estimates made near average experience, i.e. near the point of sample means.

An implicit assumption is that $x_{i, T+1}$ is known with certainty and is not subject to error. In practice this is highly questionable.

We do not know what value to assign to e_{T+1} for the unobserved forecast period; therefore we assign it an expected value of zero. If we had external information that it should be non-zero, we could assign a specific non-zero value, or we could place it in a range determined, in part, by the size of its variance. The *point* estimate for $e_{T+1} = 0$, has been called non-stochastic prediction above. Perhaps this is a poor expression since there is still a stochastic contribution made from the uncertain knowledge of the coefficients, but we behave in forecast practice as though the coefficients were known and as though errors were zero. This is why we call such extrapolations non-stochastic predictions.

Forecast bands

$$y_{T+1}^f \pm k_\gamma \delta \; S_{y_{T+1}^f}$$

can be constructed in the form of a tolerance interval to show

26

the probability γ that the bands will include the fraction δ of future observations of y_t in repeated application.[1]

The example given is simple and special. It covers only single period prediction — from sample period $t = 1, 2, \ldots, T$ to post-sample period $T + 1$. The procedure would in this case be the same if predictions were to be made for $T + 2$, $T + 3$, etc.

If we generalize the model, however, to include lagged endogenous variables as well as exogenous variables in the prediction equation, the problem becomes more complicated. The basic equation is now generalized to be

$$y_t = \sum_{i=1}^{p} a_i y_{t-i} + \sum_{i=1}^{m} \beta_i x_{it} + e_t.$$

In period $T + 1$, we can assume that y_T, y_{T-1}, y_{T-2}, etc. are known as sample observations, and the appropriate standard error formula is

$$S^2_{y_{T+1}^f} = \sum_{i,j} S_{\hat{a}_i \hat{a}_j} y_{T+1-i} y_{T+1-j} + \sum_{i,j} S_{\hat{a}_i \hat{\beta}_j} y_{T+1-i} x_{j, T+1}$$

$$+ \sum_{i,j} S_{\hat{\beta}_i \hat{\beta}_j} x_{i, T+1} x_{j, T+1} + S^2_e.$$

The change in the situation comes in the second period of prediction. Now we must use »noisy« input in order to predict output. The prediction equation is

$$y_{T+2}^f = \hat{a}_1 y_{T+1}^f + \sum_{i=2}^{p} \hat{a}_i y_{T+2-i} + \sum_{i=1}^{m} \hat{\beta}_i x_{i, T+2}.$$

1. For construction of tolerance intervals in prediction theory see W. A. Wallis, »Tolerance Intervals for Linear Regression», *Second Berkeley Symposium on Mathematical Statistics and Probability*, ed. by J. Neyman (Berkeley and Los Angeles, Univ. of Calif. Press, 1951).

In all applications, there is the possibility that $x_{i,\,T+j}$ are known only imperfectly for the prediction period, but for simplicity, we might assume that values of the independent variables are known with certainty. This can also be true of y_T, y_{T-1}, y_{T-2}, etc., but it cannot be true of y_{T+1}, which is the first lag value needed for estimation of y_{T+2}. In ex-post prediction we can observe y_{T+1} and use the correct value, but it is in the nature of ex-ante prediction that we must develop our successive lags as the extrapolation goes forward by more than one period. We must account simultaneously for the variability in $\hat{a}_1$ and in y_{T+1}^f. In addition to the usual terms in the formula for standard error of forecast, we need, ignoring second order terms involving the products of two variances,

$$\hat{a}_1^2 \, S_{y_{T+1}^f}^2 + \sum_{i=2}^{p} S_{\hat{a}_i} \, y_{T+1}^f \, \hat{a}_1 \, y_{T+2-i} + \sum_{i=1}^{m} S_{\hat{\beta}_i} \, y_{T+1}^f \, \hat{a}_1 \, x_{i,\,T+2}.$$

In ordinary regression-type calculations, some of these terms are not usually evaluated. Even if the exogenous variables are assumed to be stochastic, their covariation with the estimated coefficients would be expected to be zero. That is not so in the case of lagged dependent variables. We defer, for the moment, the more complicated calculation of appropriate formulas for standard error of forecast in the general case.

Another deficiency in the formulas is that the forecast equations actually used are *reduced forms* from a more complete system. In this case the coefficients are rows of

$$-\hat{A}_o^{-1} \sum_{i=1}^{p} \hat{A}_i \quad \text{and} \quad -\hat{A}_o^{-1} \hat{B}.$$

These estimates are obtained for structural equations with identifying restrictions and the covariances calculated are those

28

for elements of $\hat{A}_o$, $\hat{A}_t$, and $\hat{B}$. One problem is to show how these covariance estimates can be used to obtain approximate covariance estimates for the reduced form parameters. This problem has been treated by Goldberger, Nagar and Odeh.[1] They deal with the error of single period prediction, and their formulas can be translated into terms of the present exposition by assuming $A_i = 0$, $i = 1, 2, \ldots, p$. We could obtain the same result by redefining the list of independent variables to include lagged dependent variables according to the formula

$$\sum_{i=1}^{p} A_i \, y_{t-i} + B \, x_t = \Gamma z_t$$

with

$$(A_1 A_2 \ldots A_p B) = \Gamma = \begin{pmatrix} a_{111} \cdots a_{1n1} \cdots a_{11p} \cdots a_{1np} \, \beta_{11} \cdots \beta_{1m} \\ \cdot \quad\quad \cdot \quad\quad \cdot \quad\quad \cdot \quad \cdot \quad\quad \cdot \\ \cdot \quad\quad \cdot \quad\quad \cdot \quad\quad \cdot \quad \cdot \quad\quad \cdot \\ \cdot \quad\quad \cdot \quad\quad \cdot \quad\quad \cdot \quad \cdot \quad\quad \cdot \\ a_{n11} \cdots a_{nn1} \cdots a_{n1p} \cdots a_{nnp} \, \beta_{n1} \cdots \beta_{nm} \end{pmatrix}$$

$$z_t = \left[(y_{1, t-1}, \ldots, y_{n, t-1}, \ldots, y_{1, t-p}, \ldots, y_{n, t-p}, x_{1t}, \ldots, x_{mt}) \right]'$$

For simplicity, therefore, the present exposition will center on the model

$$A y_t + B x_t = e_t.$$

with reduced form

1. A. S. Goldberger, A. L. Nagar, and H. S. Odeh, »The Covariance Matrices of Reduced Form Coefficients and of Forecasts for a Structural Econometric Model», *Econometrica*, 29 (October, 1961), 556—73. See also T. M. Brown, »Standard Errors of Forecast of a Complete Econometric Model», *Econometrica*, 22 (April, 1954), 178—92.

$$y_t = \Pi x_t + v_t$$

$$\Pi = -A^{-1} B$$

$$v_t = A^{-1} e_t$$

Consider an estimate $\hat{\Pi}$ of the reduced form equation system. The covariance matrix of forecast error is

$$S^{2f}_{y_{T+1}} = F_{T+1} \, \Omega_\pi \, F'_{T+1} + \Sigma_v$$

$$F_{T+1} =$$

$$\begin{pmatrix}
x_{1,\,T+1} \cdots x_{m,\,T+1} & 0 & \cdots 0 & \cdots 0 & \cdots 0 \\
0 & \cdots 0 & x_{1,\,T+1} \cdots x_{m,\,T+1} \cdots 0 & & \cdots 0 \\
\cdot & \cdot & \cdot & \cdot & \cdot \\
\cdot & \cdot & \cdot & \cdot & \cdot \\
\cdot & \cdot & \cdot & \cdot & \cdot \\
0 & \cdots 0 & 0 & \cdots 0 & \cdots x_{1,\,T+1} \cdots x_{m,\,T+1}
\end{pmatrix}$$

$$\Omega_\pi = \begin{pmatrix}
\Omega_{11} \cdots \Omega_{1n} \\
\cdot \qquad \cdot \\
\cdot \quad \Omega_{ij} \quad \cdot \\
\cdot \qquad \cdot \\
\Omega_{n1} \cdots \Omega_{nn}
\end{pmatrix}$$

$$\Sigma_v = \begin{pmatrix}
E v_{1t}^2 \cdots E v_{1t} v_{nt} \\
\cdot \qquad \cdot \\
\cdot \qquad \cdot \\
\cdot \qquad \cdot \\
E v_{nt} v_{1t} \cdots E v_{nt}^2
\end{pmatrix}$$

F_{T+1} is an $n \times nm$ matrix display of the exogenous variables at forecast period $T + 1$; Ω_π is an $mn \times mn$ covariance matrix of estimated reduced form coefficients;[1] and Σ_v is an $n \times n$ covariance matrix of reduced form disturbances.

For evaluation of $S^{2f}_{y_{T+1}}$, we need expressions for estimates of Ω_π and Σ_v. In principle, the latter can be readily determined by computing reduced form residuals. From estimates $\hat{A}$ and $\hat{B}$ we can derive

$$\hat{\Pi} = -\hat{A}^{-1}\hat{B},$$

with all identifying restrictions taken into account. Residuals are defined by

$$y_t - \hat{\Pi}x_t = \text{res.}_t.$$

The sample covariance matrix of res.$_t$ provides an estimate of Σ_v. We can also express this as

$$\Sigma_v = A^{-1}\Sigma_e(A^{-1})'$$

which is estimated as

$$\hat{\Sigma}_v = \hat{A}^{-1}\hat{\Sigma}_e(\hat{A}^{-1})'.$$

In this expression, Σ_e is the covariance matrix of the original disturbances before transformation to reduced forms.

The problem then is to express Ω_π in terms of Ω_{AB}, the covariance matrix of the estimates of the structural parameters in A and B. To do this, we use a general asymptotic formula that expresses the covariance matrix of one set of random variables in terms of the covariance matrix of a functionally related set. Let the functional relationships be

---

1. Each element of $\Omega_\pi = (\Omega_{ij})$ is an $m \times m$ covariance matrix asso-- ciating variation of parameter estimates in one reduced form equation with variation of those in another.

$$z_i = f_i (w_1, \ldots, w_m) \qquad i = 1, 2, \ldots, n$$

and

$$\lim_{T \to \infty} E\, w_i = r_i; \quad \lim_{T \to \infty} T\, E[(w-r)(w-r)'] = \Sigma_w.$$

Then

$$\lim_{T \to \infty} T\, E[\,(z-f(r_1, \ldots, r_m))\,(z-f(r_1, \ldots, r_m))'\,] = D\, \Sigma_w\, D'$$

where

$$D = \left(\frac{\partial f_i}{\partial w_j}\right)_{w\,=\,r}.$$

If we apply this result, for large samples, to the problem of relating the covariance matrix of reduced form coefficients to structural coefficients we obtain[1]

$$\Omega_\pi = G\Omega_{AB}\, G'$$

$$G = A^{-1} \otimes (\Pi\, I) = \begin{pmatrix} a^{11}\, (\Pi\, I) \ldots a^{1n}\, (\Pi\, I) \\ \cdot \qquad\qquad \cdot \\ \cdot \qquad\qquad \cdot \\ \cdot \qquad\qquad \cdot \\ a^{n1}\, (\Pi\, I) \ldots a^{nn}\, (\Pi\, I) \end{pmatrix}.$$

Using sample estimates of Π and A ($\hat{\Pi}$ and $\hat{A}$), we can obtain an estimate of G. The estimation procedures for computing structural equation coefficients will give us estimates of Ω_{AB}; we therefore have

1. See A. S. Goldberger, A. L. Nagar, and H. S. Odeh, *op.cit.* pp. 558—61.

$$\hat{\Omega}_\pi = \hat{G}\hat{\Omega}_{AB}\,\hat{G}'.$$

Together with $\hat{\Sigma}_v$, we have enough information to estimate $S^2_{y_{T+1}^f}$.

If maximum likelihood methods are used to estimate A, B, and Σ_e, we have a means for estimating directly the full matrix Ω_{AB}, i.e. the covariance matrix for all structural coefficients in the system, within and between equations. It is not evident, however, how we should estimate the covariances between coefficients in different equations when they are estimated by a single equation method such as two-stage-least-squares, or limited-information-maximum likelihood. In this case, we can use a result of Theil that gives the estimated covariance matrix for coefficients in pairs of structural equations.[1]

$$\hat{\sigma}_{e_i}{}^j \lim_{T\to\infty} TE\left[\begin{pmatrix}\hat{Y}_i'\hat{Y}_i & \hat{Y}_i'X_i\\ X_i'\hat{Y}_i & X_i'X_i\end{pmatrix}^{-1}\begin{pmatrix}\hat{Y}_i'\hat{Y}_j & \hat{Y}_i'X_j\\ X_i'\hat{Y}_j & X_i'X_j\end{pmatrix}\begin{pmatrix}\hat{Y}_j'\hat{Y}_j & \hat{Y}_j'X_j\\ X_j'\hat{Y}_j & X_j'X_j\end{pmatrix}^{-1}\right]$$

$\hat{\sigma}_{e_{ij}}$ is the estimated covariance between e_i and e_j. It is the (i,j)-element of $\hat{\Sigma}_e$ and can be computed from the sample residuals.

Data matrices are denoted, as usual, by

$$Y = \begin{pmatrix} y_{11}\cdots y_{n1}\\ y_{12}\cdots y_{n2}\\ \cdot \qquad \cdot\\ \cdot \qquad \cdot\\ \cdot \qquad \cdot\\ y_{1T}\cdots y_{nT} \end{pmatrix}; \quad X = \begin{pmatrix} x_{11}\cdots x_{m1}\\ x_{12}\cdots x_{m2}\\ \cdot \qquad \cdot\\ \cdot \qquad \cdot\\ \cdot \qquad \cdot\\ x_{1T}\cdots x_{mT} \end{pmatrix}.$$

1. H. Theil, *Economic Forecasts and Policy*, (North-Holland Publishing Co., 1958) p. 341.

Y_i is a submatrix of Y and X_i a submatrix of X, including in both cases, only the variables appearing with non-zero coefficients in the i-th equation. $\hat{Y}_i$ are values of Y_i computed from the reduced forms.

Using a small model estimated for the period between the two wars (1921—41), Goldberger, Nagar, and Odeh evaluated ex-post forecasts and elements of $S^{2f}_{y_{1948}}$ for the post sample year, 1948. Appropriate lagged values and correct values of exogenous variables for 1948 were used. The results are given in Table 1.

Table I. Forecasts and Error, 1948

	Observation	Prediction	Error	Standard error of forecast, $S^f_{y_{1948}}$
Consumption	82.8	78.2	4.6	7.6
Investment	6.4	9.3	— 2.9	5.8
Wage bill	60.7	59.9	0.8	7.1
Profits	27.9	27.2	0.8	7.2
National income	97.4	95.7	1.7	12.6
Capital stock	204.1	207.0	— 2.9	5.8

Having the estimates of $S^f_{y_{1948}}$, we have a basis for judging the magnitude of the forecast errors. In this tiny example the forecast errors are comparatively small in terms of judgements that are often made at the macroeconomic level, but they are also small in relation to the standard error of forecast.[1] On the other

1. Given that the sample refers only to the prewar period and the interval between 1941 and 1948 is both long and highly disturbed, the ability of the model to predict as well as it does in this situation is noteworthy.

hand, the standard error of forecast is large in relation to the size of the variables being predicted. One standard error of forecast for national income is more than 10 per cent of the level of income, and this is large for applied purposes. We need to be able to predict national income consistently with error less than 5 per cent. Perhaps a larger sample as is now available will improve the estimated sampling errors of coefficients, but it is my personal conviction that the standard error of forecast can best be reduced to a level commensurate with present forecast objectives by building a larger, more realistic, and more complicated model. There are limits to the extent by which $S^{2f}_{y_{T+j}}$ can be reduced in a small system, interrelating a limited set of variables. The principal virtue of the present calculations is that they have pedagogical merit by showing how $S^{2f}_{y_{T+j}}$ should be evaluated.

The Goldberger, Nagar, Odeh contribution is very significant, but it has limited applicability. The calculations are formidable and depend to a large extent, on linearity. The problem is to seek an alternative way to evaluate the standard error of forecast more efficiently and more generally.

Let us consider the general nonlinear model

$$f_i(y_{1t}, \ldots, y_{nt}, y_{1,\ t-1}, \ldots, y_{n,\ t-p}, x_{1t}, \ldots, x_{mt}) = e_t$$

$$i = 1, 2, \ldots, n.$$

This system depends on parameters that we shall assume to have been estimated by some consistent method such as two-stage-least-squares or some variant of it. Even though the system is nonlinear, each individual equation may be linear in the parameters, after suitable transformation of variables, and this will enable us to compute $TSLS$ estimates readily. If the nonlinear-

35

ities are more substantial, it is still possible to use methods of nonlinear estimation to compute the whole set of parameters.[1]

Among the sample parameter estimates, there will be estimates of the variance-covariance matrix Σ_e. We may draw a fresh set of random errors, say normal variables, having the same covariance matrix as the sample estimate Σ_e. For the actual observations on exogenous variables over the sample period

$$x_{i1}, x_{i2}, \ldots, x_{iT}, \quad i = 1, 2, \ldots, m.$$

the sample parameter estimates, and the hypothetical random errors, we can solve the nonlinear equation system by the iteration methods outlined previously. This will give us a »pseudo sample»

$$y_{i1}^{(s)}, y_{i2}^{(s)}, \ldots, y_{iT}^{(s)} \quad i = 1, 2, \ldots, n$$

of dependent variables. The solution could be obtained in different ways:

(1) From fixed initial conditions

$$y_{i,-1}, y_{i,-2}, y_{i,-p} \quad i = 1, 2, \ldots, n$$

the system can be solved sequentially to generate the »pseudo sample».

(2) The initial conditions can be re-set every period to have the correct values of $y_{i,t-j}$. This is the assumption that underlies the received theory of estimation.

(3) The initial conditions can be re-set periodically to cover spans as long as typical forecasts.

1. See H. Eisenpress and J. Greenstadt, »The Estimation of Nonlinear Econometric Systems», *Econometrica* 34 (October, 1966), 851—61.

From the »pseudo samples« of $y_{it}^{(s)}$ and the observed x_{it} we can re-estimate the parameters of the structural system. This re-estimation can be repeated many times, each time with a new pseudo sample. We shall then have S numerical systems

$$f_i^{(s)} (y_{1t}, \ldots, y_{nt}, y_{1,\,t-1}, \ldots, y_{n,\,t-p}, x_{1t}, \ldots, x_{mt}) = 0$$

$$s = 1, 2, \ldots S.$$

Now we shall consider a forecast period outside the sample. It can be a single period or a sequence

$$t = T + 1, T + 2, T + 3, \ldots$$

For the prediction period, a given set of exogenous variables will be chosen, given initial conditions will be fixed and a fresh set of random errors, each having covariance matrix $\hat{\Sigma}_e$, will be chosen for each numerical model. The iteration method for nonlinear systems will then be used to produce predictions

$$y_{i,\,T+1}^{(s)f}, y_{i,\,T+2}^{(s)f}, \ldots \qquad \begin{array}{l} i = 1, 2, \ldots, n \\ s = 1, 2, \ldots, S \end{array}$$

We shall have S prediction sequences of each variable, one from each estimated model. An estimate of the standard error of forecast will be

$$Sy_{i,\,T+j}^f = \sqrt{\frac{1}{S} \sum_{s=1}^{S} (y_{i,\,T+j}^{(s)f} - y_{i,\,T+j}^f)^2}$$

This is the root mean square of the set of S predictions for the i-th variable about the reference prediction from the actual sample. In generating this error measure, we have jointly taken into account nonlinearity, coefficient variability, magnitude of exogenous variables, superimposed random error, and cumulation of error in sequential prediction solution. By this numerical method we should be able to obtain a complete build-up of forecast error. This method has not yet been applied to large realistic situations, but a research project of this nature is now being undertaken.[1]

This discussion completes the present stage of analysis of the first point of view on prediction error. Theoretical ranges of error can be constructed from a knowledge of the standard error of forecast. We now come to the second point of view, namely, an appropriate comparison with reality and a judgment about the goodness of forecasts. This is more a description problem, but analysis is required to choose among alternative forms of description.

Ex-ante forecasts cannot be judged one way or the other at the time of prediction, but they can eventually be judged as time unfolds the actual values. Ex-post forecasts can be judged immediately because the observed values are available at the time forecasts are made. For both types of forecast, therefore, I shall assume that observations are available on the relevant dependent variables. Judgment can be made about the evolving record of ex-ante forecasts or about the available sample of ex-post forecasts. We shall assume that there are two data series; one is

$y^f_{i, T+1}, y^f_{i, T+2}, \ldots, y^f_{i, T+F}$; forecast values, and the other is

$y_{i, T+1}, y_{i, T+2}, \ldots, y_{i, T+F}$; observed values.

Various descriptive measures have been suggested. Some are

1. The project is being carried out by Mr. George Schink of the Wharton School Econometric Forecasting Unit.*

(a) $y^f_{i, t+j} = a + b\, y_{i, t+j} + (\text{res.})_{i, t+j}$ $j = 1, 2, \ldots, F$

(b) R.M.S. error $= \sqrt{\dfrac{\displaystyle\sum_{j=1}^{F} (y^f_{i, t+j} - y_{i, t+j})^2}{F}}$

(c) Av. abs. error $= \dfrac{\displaystyle\sum_{j=1}^{F} \left| y^f_{i, t+j} - y_{i, t+j} \right|}{F}$

(d) $U = \sqrt{\dfrac{\Sigma (\Delta y^f_{i, t+j} - \Delta y_{i, t+j})^2}{\Sigma (\Delta y_{i, t+j})^2}}$

The first of these measures is a regression of predicted on actual values. Goodness of prediction is measured by the magnitude of the correlation between $y^f_{i, t+j}$ and $y_{i, t+j}$ and by the differences $|a - o|$, $|b - 1|$. Perfect scores would be indicated by unit correlation $(\text{res.}_{i, t+j} = o)$ with $a = o$, $b = 1$. Various descriptions can be obtained from the distribution of the residuals over the $(y^f_{i, t+j}; y_{i, t+j})$ -plane in relation to the $45°$-line, i.e., the line of perfect prediction.

The root-mean-square error in (b) or the average absolute error in (c) would be zero if there were perfect scores in measure (a). They show departures from the $45°$-line, in some average sense. These two measures can be made more meaningful if they are expressed as ratios to actual values $y_{i, t+j}$, to historical mean values of $y_{i, t}$, to average absolute first differences of $y_{i, t}$, or to the historical standard deviation of $y_{i, t}$.

The measure in (d) is a goodness-of-fit statistic that assumes the value 0 when prediction is perfect and is 1 when the predicted change has the same *RMS* error as »no-change» extrapolation. The denominator is the square root of the mean square successive difference. The measure U is Theil's inequality coefficient.[1] The same kind of measure could be used for accuracy of predictions of levels, but Theil develops this measure for prediction of changes.

From another view point, we may compare tolerance intervals of prediction

$$y^f_{i,\,t+j} \pm k_{\gamma\delta}\ S y^f_{i,\,t+j}$$

with actual values. If δ per cent of actual values lie in this interval, we may conclude that we have predicted as well as the underlying model and sample justify. In practice, however, prediction accuracy requirements by users are generally stricter than would be suggested by the theoretical evaluation of an interval (or multidimensional region). This approach is perhaps more useful in the detection of structural change. The purely descriptive measures of prediction accuracy are likely to be found more useful to the people who must base their decisions on predictions.

Some students have strong preferences for one descriptive measure or another. They all tend to measure the same phenomena, and it is hard to make a priori judgments about particular descriptive statistics. The mean absolute percentage error is so intuitively obvious as a measure that I would prefer it on grounds of simplicity and ease of understanding.

All these descriptive measures of forecast error fail to account properly for bias. If predictions are systematically biased —

---

1. H. Theil, *Applied Economic Forecasting*, (Amsterdam: North-Holland Publishing Co., 1966), p. 28.

always too high, or always too low, by constant or foreseeable amounts — we can readily recognize this discrepancy and improve the usefulness of predictions. In using the formula

$$y^f_{i,\ t+j} = a + b\,y_{i,\ t+j} + (\text{res.})_{i,\ t+j}$$

we may be more interested in obtaining high correlation than in the more restrictive result $a = 0$, $b = 1$. In this case, the simple correlation between $y^f_{i,\ t+j}$ and $y_{i,\,t+j}$ is the criterion by which to measure accuracy of prediction.

Having settled on the selection of some descriptive measure of forecast error, we have not yet settled the issue of judging the goodness of prediction. In the case of conditional forecasts, we should not measure the actual errors without taking into account whether the conditions that were imposed at the time of prediction actually prevailed in reality. Either the forecaster made a mistaken judgment in the setting of conditions, or actions were taken on the basis of the forecast to change conditions in a specific way and thus invalidate the forecast. If the conditioned forecast indicates an undesirable movement in the economy and if the public authorities act, on the basis of the forecast, to counter this movement, we should not conclude that successful policy implementation made the forecast inaccurate. One of the primary purposes of forecasting is to provide guides to policy makers, and the fulfillment of this purpose should not figure as a score against the prediction record.

It would seem that it would be easy enough to guard against misjudgment of forecast accuracy by confining the measurement of error to ex-post forecasts in which corrected initial conditions and correct values of exogenous variables are used in the prediction equations. This does not settle the matter, however, for ex-ante predictions. The issue is the following: *What would have been the ex-ante prediction, at the beginning of the prediction period, if subsequent knowledge about initial conditions, exogenous variables, and parameter changes had been known on the earlier occasion?* It does not follow that it would have simply been the mechanical ex-post forecast obtained by substituting the corrected initial conditions and correct exogenous variables into the equation system. As I shall argue in the next section, mechanistic predictions can be improved upon. In any realistic forecast situation, we rely on recent historical error trends, and a priori (expert) information about special events to make parametric adjustments to an estimated model just prior to ex-ante prediction. We must re-examine, in retrospect, what parametric changes would have been made in conjunction with the new information about lags and exogenous variables in simulating the ex-ante forecast exercise. This is by no means a trivial problem. It can be approximated, in practice but has not, to my knowledge, ever been done on a proper scale for evaluating ex-ante forecasts. It is an important research task because statistical series are constantly being revised by large amounts. Overall *GNP* measures may change as much as 10 per cent in successive revisions. More often the change is no more than 1 per cent in the major magnitudes but this is as large an error as can be tolerated in many policy decisions. Components of *GNP* may be revised by as much as 50 or 100 per cent. At the time of ex-ante prediction, we really do not know at what level the economy has just been performing and our future judgments of exogenous variables may be widely off the mark, partly as a result of using preliminary historical values as a basis for judging future movements.

Finally, I come to the standard against which accuracy should be judged. One of the first standards that was ever suggested was the so-called »naive model», the most obvious being the »no-change naive model»

42

$$y_{i,t} = y_{i,t-1} + e_{it}$$

The next most obvious case is

$$y_{i,t} - y_{i,t-1} = y_{i,t-1} - y_{i,t-2} + e_{it}$$

But these »obvious» cases could be extended indefinitely, and there are an unlimited number of »naive» models that no responsible person is willing to accept as a basis for economic decision making. It seems to be an exceedingly poor standard of reference. So much of modern econometric work outperforms a variety of these »naive models», and it hardly seems worth while to use them as standards of reference.

A model that is mechanistic, but not »naive» in the sense that it requires some statistical analysis is the pure autoregressive model

$$y_{it} = \sum_{j=1}^{p} a_{ij} y_{i,t-j} + e_{it}.$$

In this model, the researcher must determine estimates of a_{ij} and decide on a value for p on the basis of sample data. Predictions from this pure autoregressive scheme are then used as a standard of comparison. This may be a sensible standard, but there is little uniqueness in that the problem of an optimum choice of p has not been settled.

Two alternative reference standards seem to me to be preferable. A consensus of non-econometric, quantitative predictions by professional forecasters would appear to be one reasonable standard. These statistics may not be available in all places, but for the United States, the Federal Reserve Bank of Philadelphia has maintained a record of more than 50 annual forecasts of main economic magnitudes for several years. Mean predictions

43

from the Federal Reserve sample collection serve as a typical reference standard of the sort that I have in mind.

Another possible error standard, suggested to me by E. P. Howrey, is the difference between preliminary and final values published by the official data gathering agency. Since the econometrician and the official statistician are both trying to predict the same final total, we might argue that the statistician who has preliminary knowledge of the ingredients of the final total and is willing to release a figure for public use can make a good prediction (ex-post) that should serve as a reference standard in accuracy terms for the (ex-ante) econometric forecaster. H. O. Stekler has provided measures of the accuracy of a number of preliminary estimates.[1]

To give an idea of the accuracy of a repeated set of ex-ante forecasts in comparison with a standard provided by a non-econometric consensus, I present some results of the annual *GNP* predictions made from the Wharton Econometric Forecasting Model and the corresponding tabulations made by the Federal Reserve Bank of Philadelphia.

Table II. Comparisons of Annual *GNP* Forecasts *
(ex-ante, billions of current dollars)

	Observed	Wharton-EFU Model[2]	Error	Federal Reserve Tabulation, Average	Error
1963	584	585	1	573	— 11
64	623	625	2	616	— 7
65	666	662	— 4	656	— 10
66	732	728	— 4	725	— 7
67	781	784	3	785	4
Average absolute error			2.8		7.8

This table requires commentary and evaluation. The forecast situation, ex-ante, is as follows: In December of year $t - 1$ ($t =$ 1963, 1964, 1965, 1966, 1967), the data available enable us to estimate GNP for $t - 1$. This estimate is based on 3 quarters of revised preliminary estimates and a pre-preliminary estimate of the 4th quarter. The first preliminary estimate of a quarter is available approximately 3 weeks after the quarter's end and is revised a month later. In July of each year, the final revised estimate of the preceding calendar year is published. Every few years, the whole series of data are comprehensively revised.

The Wharton-EFU predictions are made, by quarters, for a period 8 quarters ahead at the end of the first month of every quarter. These are revised in subsequent calculations during the remainder of the quarter. In December of each year, a special attempt is made to give final revisions of the 4th quarter (and 7 future quarters) predictions, with the coming calendar year's estimates obtained by averaging results over four quarters, $t + 1/4, t + 2/4, t + 3/4, t + 4/4$. The 4th quarter is designated as t, and initial conditions come from the 3rd and previous quarters.

The Federal Reserve Bank of Philadelphia surveys a large collection of forecasts, presumably not econometrically based (with a very small number of exceptions), stating predicted

1. H. O. Stekler, »Data Revisions and Economic Forecasting», *Journal of the American Statistical Association*, 62 (June, 1967), 470—83.

2. A description of the Model is contained in M. K. Evans and L. R. Klein, *The Wharton Econometric Forecasting Model*, (Philadelphia: Wharton School of Finance and Commerce, University of Pennsylvania, 1968). The figures on forecast records are taken from F. G. Adams and M. K. Evans, »Econometric Forecasting with the Wharton Model», *Business Economics*, III (Spring, 1968).

values for the subsequent calendar year. The known facts to the forecasters are preliminary estimates of year $t-1$ (and earlier periods) during the final quarter of the year and private assumptions about exogenous developments during the year t.

In Table II, I have not listed the presently published GNP estimates. I have listed, from the Adams—Evans tables, values of GNP for year $t-1$, known in December of $t-1$, plus the actual change based on revised data. This is a very superficial attempt to account for data revision. It is not the same thing as listing the final revised series and comparting these with *predictions that would have been made if the forecasters had known revised initial conditions and correct exogenous variables at time $t-1$.* With the Federal Reserve tabulations, it is nearly impossible to reconstruct the decisions that would have been made. With the Wharton-EFU predictions it is possible to try to simulate the ex-ante forecast situation; the appropriate study has not yet been carried out.[1] The actual ex-ante forecasts are compared with GNP data, adjusted as explained above.

On this naive model test the formal model predictions turn out to have relatively good accuracy. On absolute standards, an annual error of less than $ 3.0 billion on average would be useful to people who rely on macroeconomic information in their decision processes. There is no known consistent body of ex-ante information that claims to this level of accuracy. Of course, a five-year record is not adequate for making final judgment about accuracy of econometric models; it is simply a consistent record of one series of attempts. GNP forecasting, as I shall discuss later, is not a complete objective by itself. The

1. Y. Haitovsky of the National Bureau of Economic Research and M. K. Evans of the Wharton School Econometric Forecasting Unit are conducting a study of ex-post forecasts with corrected inputs. *

reader is referred to the paper by Adams and Evans for a fuller analysis of prediction of other variables in the model.[1] The effects of data revision are not minor. In Table III are the final revised figures for *GNP* alongside the adjusted values used for the evaluation in Table II. The changes are quite large and comparison of ex-ante prediction with the actual values would make little sense in several instances.

Table III. Adjusted and Revised *GNP* Series
(billions of current dollars)

	December estimate plus actual change	Revised series
1963	584	591
64	623	632
65	666	684
66	732	743
67	781	785

All revised *GNP* series for year *t* have been published as July (t + 1)' final revisions except the value for 1967.

1. See also M. K. Evans and L. R. Klein, »Experience with Econometric Analysis of the American 'Konjunktur' Position», paper presented at the international conference *Is the Business Cycle Obsolete?*, London, England, 1967.

In this paper we present ex-post predictions over the sample period. They are somewhat larger than the ex-ante predictions cited here because no adjustments are made for recognizable errors in individual equations (see below, p. 50). The ex-post prediction errors from the model of the U. S. Department of Commerce do incorporate such adjustments, and their errors are of the same order of magnitude as our actual ex-ante errors. See M. Liebenberg, A. Hirsch, and J. Popkin, »A Quarterly Econometric Model of the United States: A Progress Report», *Survey of Current Business*, (May, 1966), 13—39.

THE IMPROVEMENT OF PREDICTION

The techniques of prediction have been presented here as though they involved only the solution of simultaneous numerical equation systems, in particular, econometric equation systems. One of the purposes of the present essay and associated research work on prediction theory is to introduce objective methods and eliminate personal judgment as much as possible — to emphasize the scientific over the artistic aspects of economic prediction. It would be nice to claim that economic prediction has been made into an objective, scientific discipline in which all practitioners would agree, given external conditions and specified initial values. It would be nice if any one forecaster's results could be duplicated by another and if techniques could be readily passed on from generation to generation. This rosy situation does not exist. A purely mechanistic approach to economic prediction does not exist. This does not mean that objective principles have not been attained. It means that judgment has some role to play; that purely mechanistic methods of prediction are bound to fail; and that an econometric model is an objective framework into which judgmental information may be placed.

It is self-evident that objective agreement may not be reached on future values for exogenous variables. This is an important source of personal variability in ex-ante prediction. But for any given set of judgments, predictions are objective, and often there are accepted ranges of alternatives within which choices of exogenous variables should be made.

The treatment of special information on singular events and the assignment of values to residuals in prediction is a more difficult problem, and there is no evident objective agreement. If the list of exogenous variables does not cover variation in some major event that appears to be imminent or in some discernible disturbance to the economy, the forecaster would be foolish to ignore such events or disturbances and proceed as though the sample estimates of a model, with mean residuals fixed at zero, were to hold good for the prediction period. In using the Wharton-EFU Model for prediction, we regularly make two classes of adjustment that contribute substantially to the improvement of predictive power. (1) Prior to each quarter's forecast exercise, we evaluate the residual variation in each equation of the model over the past few quarters — roughly six. If residual variation appears to be non-random and if a priori economic explanation can be adduced for the existence and continuation of this non-random character, we assign non-zero values to residuals in the prediction period. These may be means or recent values of residuals. In linear equations, this amounts to calculation of

$$(\text{res.})_{iT}, \ (\text{res.})_{i, T-1}, \ \ldots, \ (\text{res.})_{i, T-5}$$

from

$$(\text{res.})_{it} = \sum_{j=1}^{n} \sum_{k=0}^{p} \hat{a}_{ijk} \, y_{j, t-k} + \sum_{j=1}^{m} \hat{\beta}_{ij} \, x_{jt}$$

Instead of assuming

$$(\text{res.})_{i, T+j} = 0$$

we assume

$$(\text{res.})_{i, T+j} = 1/6 \sum_{k=0}^{5} (\text{res.})_{i, T-k}$$

or some other a priori plausible function of recent observations.

49

Such adjustments start the prediction calculations with the system approximately on track for the initial period. These adjustments may be necessitated by data revision between sample and prediction period as well as by the occurrence of singular events. The adjustment may be looked upon as an assignment of a non-zero value to the residuals or as a change in the value of a parameter, namely, the constant term of an equation. In the i-th equation, above, one of the variables may be unity for all t

$$y_{i,t} = 1:$$

then the constant term is $\hat{a}_{iio}$, and we may look upon the equation as one with zero values assigned to the residuals but with changed constant

$$\hat{a}_{iio} - (\text{res.})_{i,\,T+j}.$$

As data are revised, behavior changes, or unforeseen variables begin to affect the economy's performance, the whole set of parameters should be re-estimated. This is too much to ask in a system that is being used regularly for quarterly predictions. Every few years, there may be comprehensive re-estimation, but not every quarter; therefore the scheme of a priori adjustment of constant terms is used to keep a given model in very close touch with reality on an updated basis. (2) Other structural changes occur for known legislative or institutional reasons. These are changes in tax parameters, transfer payment parameters, monetary control parameters. These must be changed regularly to keep a system up to date. In addition there are »inside information» and »latest news». After the preparation of preliminary predictions from the most recently adjusted

Wharton-EFU Model, there is a discussion of the assumptions and properties of the prediction with business and government specialists. A priori information on impending labor disputes, hedge purchasing, production bottlenecks, major economic decisions and similar phenomena are then suggested for further modification of parameter or residual values, and a revised forecast is prepared. It is of the utmost importance to incorporate this expert information. It does not destroy the econometric nature of the forecast; it improves its accuracy by the feeding-in of quantified special information to a numerical, objective system that is capable of assimilating these facts. To make a proper assimilation, the econometric model should be a structural system in order that we know where to introduce the a priori adjustments. If we were to use the reduced form, final form, solution equation or some naive model we would not know where or how to incorporate the a priori information.

In the present state of econometric knowledge, the present reliability of economic data, and the present capabilities of managing detail we are not able to construct models that can be used for ex-ante predictions for several years without continual adjustment. Immediate extrapolation just beyond the sample period may be computed for a year or two without adjustment, but experience shows that a freshly estimated system, within a year or two of careful application to prediction problems, needs as much parameter adjustment as does a system that is 4—5 years older in sample span.

The adjustment of numerical equations for non-zero values of residuals may be required as a result of the presence of serial correlation. In many instances, serial correlation in sample residuals may be indicative of expected serial correlation in forecast error. At the point of sample estimation, instead of assuming

$$E e_{it}\, e_{j,\,t-k} = 0, \qquad\qquad k \neq 0$$

it may be more realistic to assume

$$e_{it} = \sum_{j=1}^{q} \varrho_{ij}\, e_{i,\,t-j} + u_{it}$$

$$E\, u_{it}\, u_{j,\,t-k} = 0, \qquad k \neq 0.$$

The autoregressive assumption can be generalized to permit cross-lag regression between e_{it} and $e_{j,\,t-k}$, but our capabilities have not extended beyond the treatment of the *auto*regressive case displayed above. In practice, we find that $q = 0, 1, 2$ seem to be adequate for empirical relationships. It is worth pointing out that $q = 2$ is a frequently required specification with quarterly economic data.

It is well known that linear equations with autoregressive errors preserve their parametric form in terms of transformed variables

$$y'_{j,\,t-k} = y_{j,\,t-k} - \sum_{l=1}^{q} \varrho_{il}\, y_{j,\,t-k-l}$$

$$x'_{jt} = x_{j,\,t} - \sum_{l=1}^{q} \varrho_{il}\, x_{j,\,t-l}.$$

The transformed equation is

$$\sum_{j=1}^{n} \sum_{k=o}^{p} a_{ijk}\, y'_{j,\,t-k} + \sum_{j=1}^{m} \beta_{ij}\, x'_{jt} = u_{it}.$$

A seemingly natural and straightforward way of dealing with the extended model containing autoregressive errors is to estimate jointly the parameters a_{ijk}, β_{ij}, ϱ_{ij} and use these estimates in prediction. The problem of parameter estimation is not

52

difficult in single structural equations that split off, in recursive fashion, with only one unlagged dependent variable present. The estimates of these single equations are obtained by regressing y'_{it} on lagged and exogenous variables $(y'_{j,\,t-k}, x'_{jt})$. The two standard computing techniques are:

1. A search technique in which a constrained area of the parameter space for ϱ_{i1} and ϱ_{i2} is systematically scanned for values that minimize the residual sum of squares. The computed residuals are tested for time dependence, and it is nearly always found that a first or second order auto-regressive transformation produces seemingly random residuals. The search area is constrained so that the roots of

$$\lambda^2 - \varrho_{i1}\lambda - \varrho_{i2} = 0$$

have modulus less than unity. This is a fast computing technique.

2. An iterative procedure suggested by Cochrane and Orcutt may be used.[1] Let residuals on the s-th iteration be defined as

$$\hat{u}_{it}^{(s)} = \sum_{j=1}^{n} \sum_{k=o}^{p} \hat{a}_{ijk}^{(s)}\, y'^{(s-1)}_{j,\,t-k} + \sum_{j=1}^{m} \hat{\beta}_{ij}^{(s)}\, x'^{(s-1)}_{jt}$$

$$\hat{e}_{it}^{(s)} = \sum_{j=1}^{n} \sum_{k=o}^{p} \hat{a}_{ijk}^{(s)}\, y^{(s-1)}_{j,\,t-k} + \sum_{j=1}^{m} \hat{\beta}_{ij}^{(s)}\, x^{(s-1)}_{jt}$$

They are computed by using the regression coefficients $\hat{a}_{ijk}^{(s)}\ \hat{\beta}_{ij}^{(s)}$ estimated on the s-th iteration from transformed

1. D. Cochrane and G. H. Orcutt, »Application of Least Squares Regression to Relationships Containing Autocorrelated Error Terms», *Journal of the American Statistical Association*, 44 (March, 1949), pp. 32—61.

variables, where the transformations use $\hat{\varrho}_{i1}^{(s-1)}$ and $\hat{\varrho}_{i2}^{(s-1)}$. To obtain $\hat{\varrho}_{i1}^{(s)}$ and $\hat{\varrho}_{i2}^{(s)}$, we regress $\hat{e}_{it}^{(s)}$ on $\hat{e}_{i,\,t-1}^{(s)}$ and $\hat{e}_{i,\,t-2}^{(s)}$. Sargan has proved that this iterative process converges in the first-order case.[1]

These methods can be similarly applied to the non-recursive parts of simultaneous equation models, but the necessary details have not in fact been worked out. In *TSLS* estimation the independent variables in the first stage reduced form regressions would change for each choice of a pair $(\varrho_{i1}, \varrho_{i2})$ in the search procedure. First stage estimates of $\hat{y}_{it}$ would depend on the search values, and the appropriate ones could be used in auto-regressively transformed form in the second stage. The whole second stage equation should be transformed to be expressed in terms of $y_{j,\,t-k}'$ and x_{jt}'.

The purpose of the more refined estimation procedure in the presence of serially correlated errors is to obtain more efficient estimates of α_{ijk} and β_{ij}. Having these improved coefficient estimates, we may choose two alternative equations for prediction, either

$$\sum_{j=1}^{n}\sum_{k=o}^{p}\hat{a}_{ijk}\left(y_{j,\,t-k}-\hat{\varrho}_{i1}\,y_{j,\,t-k-1}-\hat{\varrho}_{i2}\,y_{j,\,t-k-2}\right)$$

$$+\sum_{j=1}^{m}\hat{\beta}_{ij}\left(x_{jt}-\hat{\varrho}_{i1}\,x_{j,\,t-1}-\hat{\varrho}_{i2}\,x_{j,\,t-2}\right)=o$$

or

$$\sum_{j=1}^{n}\sum_{k=o}^{p}\hat{a}_{ijk}\,y_{j,\,t-k}+\sum_{j=1}^{m}\hat{\beta}_{ij}\,x_{jt}=o.$$

1. J. D. Sargan, »Wages and Prices in the United Kingdom: A Study in Econometric Methodology«, *Proceedings of the 16th Symposium of the Colston Research Society*, (London: Butterworths, 1964).

Although it may seem obvious that it would be better to predict from the first of the two since the estimated relationships in this form have isolated independent errors, it is not a clear choice. For one period predictions, lagged values are known in each case, and the residual sum of squares over the sample period, is lower for the first than for the second. In the first order case the ratio of the population variances is $\sigma_u^2/\sigma_e^2 = (1 - \varrho^2)$. We would expect the more favorable residual pattern to carry over to the prediction period. The lag structure is, however, different between the two equations, and more lags are used in the first. In multiperiod predictions, the error build-up in using estimated values of $y_{j,\,t-k}$ could be larger in the first than in the second equation system. This error contribution may worsen the multiperiod predictions with the first equation as compared with the second. In using the second equation for prediction, we would make use of the efficient estimates of a_{ijk} and β_{ij}, but we would be developing residuals from a serially correlated process. The mechanical use of a single autoregressively transformed equation is equivalent to correcting the untransformed equation (efficiently estimated) by estimating the prediction residual from the sample autoregression of residuals.[1] The use of the untransformed equation with more selective and a priori information on residual patterns, as explained above, may turn out to be a better procedure in prediction.

This discussion leads to a broader issue — what are efficient procedures for dealing with lagged dependent variables in prediction? Apart from the problem of accounting for the error

1. For long prediction intervals, the use of a stable autoregressive process to estimate future residuals converges to the mean residual ($=$ zero), and the second equation is the limiting formula.

build-up as estimated values of lagged variables are used in multiperiod prediction, there is a further problem of estimating lag relationships in a way that leads to optimum predictions. The latter problem may be formulated this way: In estimation theory we treat lagged dependent variables as though they were predetermined, i.e. they are treated like exogenous variables. This has been justified in the case of serially independent disturbances by Mann and Wald for large samples.[1] In multiperiod ex-ante prediction, we cannot assume that lagged dependent variables are given. *Only the initial values are given.* After the first period's prediction, future values of lagged input must be endogenously generated by the model itself. There is thus a contradiction of assumptions between estimation theory and prediction theory. Intuitively, I would think that »best» predictions based only on the assumption that initial conditions and exogenous variables are given would be produced by a system that gave the »best fit» to the sample period under analogous and consistent assumptions.

Consider the simplest possible model exhibiting this problem

$$y_t = a\, y_{t-1} + e_t$$

with estimate of $a = a$. Prediction is given by[2]

$$y^f_{T+j} = a^j y_T,$$

while the true values are

1. H. B. Mann and A. Wald, »On the Statistical Treatment of Linear Stochastic Difference Equations», *Econometrica* 11 (July—October, 1943), 173—220.

2. The optimality of this prediction formula is shown by T. Haavelmo, *The Probability Approach in Econometrics*, supplement to *Econometrica*, 12 (July, 1944), 112—13.

$$y_{T+j} = a^j y_T + \sum_{i=T+1}^{T+j} a^{T+j-i} e_i.$$

In the sample period a is chosen as an estimate of α so as to

minimize $\sum_{t=1}^{T} e_t^2$. In the forecast period, if we use mean square

error as a prediction criterion, we should seek to minimize

$$\sum_{j=1}^{F} (\sum_{i=T+1}^{T+j} a^{T+j-i} e_i)^2.$$

For large values of j, i.e. for distant predictions, the expected value of squared error becomes

$$\sigma_e^2 / (1 - a^2),$$

but the major prediction problem is for medium or short run prediction — something under 5 years. In that case, we cannot assume that j is large.

Over the whole sample period, undoubtedly longer than the maximum prediction interval, the problem of choosing a so as to minimize mean square error of prediction is to find a parameter value satisfying.[1]

---

1. In an unpublished paper, Malinvaud has pointed out that the least squares estimate of α in the model $y_t = \alpha^t y_0 + e_t$ is not consistent. Our model is, however, different because the error term is $\sum_{i=1}^{t} a^{t-i} e_i$. Moreover, consistency is not necessarily an overriding criterion in our search for optimal prediction systems. E. Malinvaud, »The Consistency of Non-Linear Regressions», Working Paper in Mathematical Economics and Econometrics No. 109, University of California, Berkeley, July, 1967. *

$$\sum_{t=1}^{T} (y_t - a^t y_o)^2 = \text{min.}$$

With only one unknown parameter, a simple search procedure would be adequate. Values of a in the interval $-1 < a < +1$ could be chosen sequentially until a value with minimal squared error were found. Alternatively, an iteration process could be developed for solving the minimization conditions

$$\sum_{t=1}^{T} t\, y_t\, a^{t-1} = y_o \sum_{t=1}^{T} t\, a^{2t-1}.$$

The finite sum on the right hand side can be expressed as

$$y_o \sum_{t=1}^{T} t\, a^{2t-1} = y_o\, \frac{a + (T-1)\, a^{2T+1} - T\, a^{2T+3}}{(1-a^2)^2}.$$

For an initial value a_o, the left hand side can be evaluated as S_o, and the next iteration value will be the root of

$$S_o = y_o\, \frac{a + (T-1)\, a^{2T+1} - T\, a^{2T+3}}{(1-a^2)^2}.$$

It should be remarked that when a is small, a^{2T+1} and a^{2T+3} may be negligible.

This procedure seeks to establish an estimate of a that minimizes the squared error along the *solution path* of the equation, given initial conditions. The entire solution path may span more than a reasonable forecast interval. A formulation for relatively short forecast intervals, $F < T$, is

$$\sum_{j=1}^{F} \sum_{t=1}^{T} (y_{t+j} - a^j y_t)^2 = \text{min.}$$

58

This has an advantage of making the estimation procedure less sensitive to a single starting value y_o.

This is not a new idea in econometrics. At an earlier stage the notion of choosing parameter estimates so as to minimize the squared error along the solution path was rejected because the solution errors are not independent and they do not admit a simple probability explanation.[1]

An alternative approach may help to clarify and justify the estimator suggested here. The simple model

$$y_t = a\, y_{t-1} + e_t \qquad t = 1, 2, \ldots, T$$

may be rewritten in solution form as

$$y_t = a^t y_o + \sum_{i=1}^{t} a^{t-i} e_i$$

$$y_t = a^t y_o + u_t .$$

Our criterion for a parameter estimate leading to optimal prediction is

$$\sum_{t=1}^{T} u_i^2 = \min.$$

We can express this as

1. Cf. T. Haavelmo, »The Inadequacy of Testing Dynamic Theory by Comparing Theoretical Solutions and Observed Cycles», *Econometrica*, 8 (October, 1940), 12—21.

$$\sum_{t=1}^{T} u_t^2 = \sum_{t=1}^{T} \left(\sum_{i=1}^{t} a^{t-i} e_i\right)^2$$

$$= \sum_{t=1}^{T} \left[e_1^2 + (a e_1 + e_2)^2 + (a^2 e_1 + a e_2 + e_3)^2 + \ldots + \right.$$

$$\left. (a^{T-1} e_1 + a^{T-2} e_2 + \ldots + e_T)^2\right] .$$

This can be rewritten, by expanding and regrouping terms, as

$$\sum_{t=1}^{T} u_t^2 = (e_1 e_2 \ldots e_T) \times$$

$$\begin{pmatrix}
(1 + a^2 + a^4 \ldots + a^{2T-2}) & (a + a^3 + \ldots + a^{2T-3}) & \ldots & a^{T-1} \\
(a + a^3 + \ldots + a^{2T-3}) & (1 + a^2 + \ldots + a^{2T-4}) & & \cdot \quad \cdot \\
\cdot & & \cdot & \cdot \quad \cdot \\
\cdot & \cdot & \cdot & \cdot \\
\cdot & & & (1 + a^2) \quad a \\
a^{T-1} & \cdot & \cdot & a \quad 1
\end{pmatrix} \times$$

$$[(e_1, e_2, \ldots, e_T)]'$$

$$\sum_{t=1}^{T} u_t^2 = e' \, \Phi \, (a) \, e .$$

The problem may now be posed as

$$e' \, \Phi \, (a) \, e = \min.$$

$$e_t = y_t - a \, y_{t-1} .$$

The ordinary least squares regression, denoted as a_1 is obtained as

$$e' \, \Phi \, (0) \, e = (y - a \, y_{-1})' \, \Phi \, (0) \, (y - a \, y_{-1}) = \min.,$$

with obvious notation

$$y'_{-1} = (y_0, y_1, y_2, \ldots, y_{T-1})$$

$$y' = (y_1, y_2, y_3, \ldots, y_T).$$

It can be expressed as

$$a_1 = \frac{\displaystyle\sum_{t=1}^{T} y_t y_{t-1}}{\displaystyle\sum_{t=1}^{T} y_{t-1}^2}.$$

This is a consistent estimate of a, but is obtained by writing $\Phi(0)$ for $\Phi(a)$. An obvious improvement is to replace $\Phi(0)$ by $\Phi(a_1)$, since a_1 is a better estimate of a than is 0.

Given this first stage estimate of $\Phi(a)$, we assume the covariance matrix Φ to be known and minimize

$$(y - a y_{-1})' \, \Phi(a_1) \, (y - a y_{-1}).$$

The solution is

$$a_2 = \frac{y'_{-1} \Phi(a_1) y}{y'_{-1} \Phi(a_1) y_{-1}}.$$

This is the usual formula for an Aitken estimator of a regression coefficient with given covariance matrix of additive error in a linear relation.

With a consistent estimator of $\Phi(a)$ in the first stage, the second stage estimate of a, denoted a_2, is also a consistent estimate.

We are tempted to iterate this process to obtain a solution to

$$(y - a y_{-1})' \, \Phi(a) \, (y - a y_{-1}) = \min,$$

61

but since both Φ and e depend on the same parameter we cannot neglect the terms obtained by varying a in Φ (a) for given values in $(y - a y_{-1})$. In analogous problems, such as the well known Cochrane—Orcutt iteration procedure mentioned above, the parameters of Φ differ from those in the linear structural relation; therefore iteration with successive linear calculations leads to minimization. In the present problem, we cannot avoid nonlinear calculations; so we may as well go to a direct solution of

$$\sum_{t=1}^{T} (y_t - a^t y_o)^2 = \text{min.}$$

The corresponding estimate when $F < T$ is

$$a_2 = \frac{\displaystyle\sum_{t=0}^{T-F} (y_t \ldots y_{t+F-1}) \, \Phi_F (a_1) \, [(y_{t+1}, \ldots, y_{t+F})]'}{\displaystyle\sum_{t=0}^{T-F} (y_t \ldots y_{t+F-1}) \, \Phi_F (a_1) \, [(y_t, \ldots, y_{t+F-1})]'}.$$

Φ_F (a) is the S.E. principal minor of Φ (a), having F rows and columns.

This alternative interpretation transforms a nonlinear estimation problem into two-stage linear calculations of generalized least squares. Since we are minimizing a quadratic form in $e_1, \ldots, e_T$, the probability interpretation of the estimates is clearer. It is also instructive in showing how the OLS estimate a_1 is altered for use in prediction by taking explicit account of the fact that the cumulated error of prediction

$$u_t = \sum_{i=1}^{t} a^{t-i} e_i$$

is not independent from period to period.

62

There is no problem in formally generalizing the present approach to the case of a single equation with many own lags and exogenous variables, or even to the solution of a complete system. The generalized single equation is

$$y_t = \sum_{i=1}^{p} a_i y_{t-i} + \sum_{j=1}^{m} \beta_j x_{jt} + e_t$$

with solution

$$y_t = \sum_{i=1}^{p} C_i \lambda_i^t + \sum_{k=1}^{t} \gamma_k \left(\sum_{j=1}^{m} \beta_j x_{jk} + e_k \right).$$

The C_i are determined by the initial conditions and the parameter values of the system; the λ_i are roots of the characteristic equation

$$\lambda^p - a_1 \lambda^{p-1} - \ldots - a_p = 0;$$

and the γ_k are functions of the parameters. Mean square prediction error

$$\sum_{t=1}^{T} \left(\sum_{k=1}^{t} \gamma_k e_k \right)^2$$

is minimized for parameter estimates of a_i and β_j that produce

$$S = \sum_{t=1}^{T} \left(y_t - \sum_{i=1}^{p} C_i \lambda_i^t - \sum_{k=1}^{t} \gamma_k \sum_{j=1}^{m} \beta_j x_{jk} \right)^2 = \text{min.}$$

The minimization process seeks structural parameter estimates and not simply estimates of the parameters in the solution form. General nonlinear methods would have to be used to solve[1]

1. See H. Eisenpress and J. Greenstadt, *op.cit.*

$$\frac{\partial S}{\partial a_i} = 0; \frac{\partial S}{\partial \beta_j} = 0.$$

As in the the explicit treatment of the first-order case, the mean square error need not be evaluated about the entire sample period solution path from $t = 1$ to $t = T$ but could be done in shorter intervals corresponding to shorter predictions.

The single-equation prediction problem can be extended to simultaneous estimation of parameters in an entire linear system from the solution form given above.

$$y_t = K \lambda^t - \frac{a(L)}{\Delta(L)} B x_t + \frac{a(L)}{\Delta(L)} e_t.$$

A criterion function would have to be constructed. Possibly the trace of

$$\sum_{t=1}^{T} v_t v_t'$$

$$v_t = \frac{a(L)}{\Delta(L)} e_t$$

should be minimized for the case in which each element of the trace is normalized by division by $\sum_{t=1}^{T} (y_{it} - \bar{y}_i)^2$.

For a nonlinear system, the solution cannot be generally expressed in closed mathematical form. Numerical solutions over the sample period can be approximated for any given set of parameter estimates, and we can seek an algorithm that minimizes an accepted error of prediction for alternative sets of parameter estimates.

Whether the system is linear or nonlinear it is difficult to form an expression for the variances and covariances of prediction error in a dynamic model as explicit functions of the structural parameters. A hopeful approach may be to use analog or hybrid computers to search for parameter combinations that minimize error, in some sense, along the solution path. The use of a computer search, mixed with other methods of estimation, by »cut-and-try» methods is given by Cohen in his industry model for shoes, leather, and hides.[1]

In all but special and simplified cases, however, the estimation of parameters in dynamic models by minimization of multiperiod prediction error is not well understood yet nor easy to execute. I do not mean to be pessimistic about our ability to treat large scale nonlinear systems. The problems involved are indeed being overcome, and the Eisenpress—Greenstadt programs have, in fact, been used in the structural estimation of a 15-equation nonlinear model. It will be possible to extend this to moderately larger systems and, eventually, to the methods that minimize multiperiod prediction error, but at this stage it seems more sensible to try to obtain the best possible structural estimates of a model by reference to accepted criteria such as maximization of the likelihood function

$$p_r \left(e_{11}, \ldots, e_{nT} \right)$$

or »best fit» of individual structural equations, by consistent methods, over the sample period. A variant of $TSLS$ methods seems to be desirable in this connection. But the process of multiperiod solution generates serial dependence of errors in

1. K. J. Cohen, *Computer Models of the Shoe, Leather, Hide Sequence* (Englewood Cliffs, N. J.: Prentice-Hall, Inc., 1960).

dynamic systems; therefore autoregressive analysis of ex-post simulated prediction errors in the sample period

$$\hat{v}_{i,\,t+j} = r_{i1}\,\hat{v}_{i,\,t+j-1} + r_{i2}\,v_{i,\,t+j-2} + \ldots$$

would seem to provide good formulas for estimating the residual to be expected in the prediction period. In the sample period we can compute numerical values of

$$\hat{v}_{i,\,t+j} = y^f_{i,\,t+j} - y_{i,\,t+j} \qquad \begin{array}{l} t = 1, \ldots, T \\[4pt] j = 1, 2, \ldots, \quad F, F < T \end{array}$$

find their empirical autoregressive structure; start with initial values, from observed data, and use as the prediction

$$y^f_{i,\,T+j} + v^f_{i,\,T+j}$$

where the correction term is found from the empirical recursive formula for $\hat{v}_{i,\,t+j}$ and initial conditions. This has not been the practice in making ex-ante predictions with the Wharton-EFU Model. In that case, adjustments for serial effects are made for structural equations on the basis of their residual performance. In this section the argument is being made that we should examine the residual performance in solution values.

A plausible approach to the problem of parameter estimation that is *consistent* with the assumptions and goals of prediction, although, not necessarily optimal, is suggested by a modification and extension of multi-stage least squares procedure proposed by Jorgenson.[1]

---

1. See R. L. Cooper and D. W. Jorgenson, »The Predictive Performance of Quarterly Econometric Models of the U.S.», Working Paper in Mathematical Economics and Econometrics, No. 113, University of California, Berkeley, August, 1967; also presented at the Bonn meetings of the Econometric Society, August, 1967.

Suppose that the standard linear model

$$\sum_{i=0}^{p} A_i y_{t-i} + B x_t = e_t$$

is estimated equation-by-equation according to the usual two-stage-least-squares *(TSLS)* procedures. Actually, Jorgenson recommends that these initial estimates be obtained by a special case of *TSLS*, namely indirect least squares. This would be equivalent to *TSLS* if the equations were *just identified*. In the usual *over identified* case it is equivalent to choosing instruments among the predetermined set of variables just equal to the number of dependent variables (less one) in the estimation of each structural equation. If there were no problems of degrees of freedom or multicollinearity, I would prefer to use the ordinary set of *TSLS* estimates in this stage, or, in the event of such complicating problems, I would prefer to use *TSLS* based on principal components, as explained below. The advantage of not using indirect least squares is that arbitrariness of selection of instruments is removed. Although asymptotic properties may not be affected, for small sample estimation it is highly desirable to obtain results that are free of personal judgment.

Having the estimated system

$$\sum_{i=0}^{p} \hat{A}_i y_{t-i} + \hat{B} x_t = 0,$$

Jorgenson obtains one-period solutions for the dependent variables in each sample period. These will be denoted as

$$\hat{\hat{y}}_t = - \hat{A}_o^{-1} \left(\sum_{i=1}^{p} \hat{A}_i y_{t-i} + \hat{B} x_t \right).$$

The notation $\hat{\hat{y}}_t$ is used here to distinguish these computed values from $\hat{y}_t$, which will be taken as computed values of y_t from *unrestricted* reduced-form regressions

$$\hat{y}_t = \hat{\Pi} z_t,$$

where z_t is the combined vector of lagged dependent variables and independent variables defined previously. There is a major difference between $\hat{\hat{y}}_t$ and $\hat{y}_t$. The latter are obtained from estimated reduced forms with no priori restrictions imposed. In the second stage of *TSLS* estimation these are used with the restrictions on single equations, one-at-a-time, to estimate structural parameters from least squares regressions. By contrast, the $\hat{\hat{y}}_t$ are obtained from estimated reduced forms *in which all the restrictions on the system* are used simultaneously. Jorgenson's final stage regressions of individual y_{it} on (non-normalized) elements of $\hat{\hat{y}}_t$ and included elements of z_t for each equation are a form of *full-information* estimates.[1] The usual *TSLS* estimates are *limited-information* estimates.

It should be remarked that Jorgenson's proposed estimators are truncated forms of iterated *TSLS* estimates originally suggested by Houthakker and reported by Theil.[2] The Houthakker suggestion was to revise successive estimates of the covariance matrix of reduced form residuals used in k-class estimation on the basis of *restricted* reduced form estimates. Jorgenson makes one such revision instead of repeated revisions, but this single revision obtains full information of a priori restrictions.

---

1. Non-normalized elements are those dependent variables in an equation with unknown coefficients or non unit coefficients. The normalized dependent variable means that one with a *unit* coefficient.

2. H. Theil, *Economic Forecasts and Policy* (Amsterdam: North-Holland Publishing Co., 1958), p. 361, fn. 1. In a later edition Theil reports (p. 355) that there is a lack of convergence in some cases.

An extension of the Jorgenson method is highly relevant for our interest in obtaining estimators for consistent and efficient prediction. If the elements of $\hat{\hat{y}}_t$ are computed dynamically from fixed initial conditions as in prediction applications, we shall then have a complete correspondence between the assumptions that underlie sample period estimation and predictive applications.

First, let us consider predictions as far forward as the sample length, $t = 1, 2, \ldots, T$. If the elements of $\hat{\hat{y}}_t$ are obtained from the *solution* of the finite difference equations,

$$\sum_{i=0}^{p} \hat{A}_i y_{t-i} + \hat{B} x_t = 0,$$

from fixed initial conditions, prior to $t = 1$, and the actual independent variables of the sample period, we then shall have $\hat{\hat{y}}_t$ as linear functions of x_t and the initial conditions. The final stage regressions using elements of $\hat{\hat{y}}_t$ and x_t as independent variables will then not make the usual assumptions that y_{t-i} are predetermined at period t.

For short predictions, $F < T$, values in $\hat{\hat{y}}_t$ would have to be determined every period, given that period's initial conditions, for the subsequent F periods; i.e., we would have

$$\hat{\hat{y}}_{1, t}, \hat{\hat{y}}_{2, t}, \ldots, \hat{\hat{y}}_{F, t}$$

based on initial values for $y_{t-1}, y_{t-2}, \ldots, y_{t-p}$. We need two subscripts on the $\hat{\hat{y}}_{j, t}$ to show, respectively, how far ahead the solution is made and from what initial point it is made.

To show how the final stage regressions would be formed in general, let us rewrite the system

$$\sum_{i=0}^{r} A_i y_{t-i} + Bx_t = e_t$$

as

$$y_t = -A_o^* y_t - \sum_{i=1}^{\nu} A_i y_{t-i} - Bx_t + e_t; \quad a_{iio}^* = 0$$

This expresses each element of y_t as a linear function of other elements in y_t, lagged values y_{t-i} $(i = 1, 2, \ldots, p)$ and independent variables x_t. In the final stage regressions we replace elements of y_t by $\hat{\hat{y}}_t$ and appropriate elements in y_{t-i} by $\hat{\hat{y}}_{t-i}$ as follows: we form one single regression for each element of y_t on

$\hat{\hat{y}}_{1,t}, \quad y_{t-i}$ $(i = 1, 2, \ldots, p)$, and x_t; $\qquad t = 1, 2, \ldots, T$

$\hat{\hat{y}}_{2,t-1}, \hat{\hat{y}}_{1,t-1}, y_{t-i}$ $(i = 2, \ldots, p)$ and x_t; $\qquad t = 2, 3, \ldots, T$

$\hat{\hat{y}}_{3,t-2}, \hat{\hat{y}}_{2,t-2}, \hat{\hat{y}}_{1,t-2}, y_{t-i}$ $(i = 3, \ldots, p)$ and x_t $\quad t = 3, 4, \ldots, T$

.

.

.

$\hat{\hat{y}}_{F,t-F+1}, \hat{\hat{y}}_{F-1,t-F+1}, \hat{\hat{y}}_{F-2,t-F+1} \cdots$ and x_t

$$t = F, F + 1, \ldots, T$$

This could be done by weighted or unweighted regression, depending on whether we want to attach some a priori significance to particular length predictions.

This estimation procedure is clear enough for linear systems, for each element of $\hat{\hat{y}}_t$ is a linear function of independent variables, initial conditions, and an additive weighted average of random errors. The probability limit of y_t is therefore a linear function of independent variables and initial conditions. It qualifies as an instrumental variable. The interpretation is not this simple in nonlinear systems.

It is easy enough to compute $\hat{\hat{y}}_t$ for nonlinear systems. We may use the algorithm (Gauss—Seidel) stated above in a previous section for solving dynamic nonlinear simultaneous equation systems.[1] This can be used in single-period solutions, as needed in the strict application of Jorgenson's procedure, or in multi-period solutions as needed in our extension of his procedure. The difficulty, however, is not in obtaining numerical solutions on the non-stochastic, nonlinear equation system. The difficulty is that such solutions are not necessarily the probability limit of $\hat{\hat{y}}_t$. In solving nonlinear equations, we cannot assert that the solution splits into two additive and independent components — one a function of exogenous variables and initial conditions, and the other a function of random errors with finite probability limit. Thus the statistical interpretation of the nonlinear extension is not clear, but in a formal sense there is little problem in carrying out the indicated calculations.

It may be worthwhile to point out some empirical findings on ex-post simulation and ex-post prediction with a particular model.[2] The model to be considered is an annual system of 20 equations, that is basically an updated and enlarged version of the so-called Klein—Goldberger Model. This system has been estimated from data spanning 1929—1941; 1947—1964. Estimates of parameters have been obtained by using ordinary least squares (OLS), two-stage-least-squares (4, 8, 12 principal components of predetermined variables) ($TSPC$ 4, 8, 12), and full-

1. Other methods such as the Newton—Raphson method could also be used.

2. The model and some empirical findings are presented in my paper, »Estimation of Interdependent Systems in Macroeconometrics», presented as the Henry Schultz Lecture at the Econometric Society meetings in Bonn, August, 1967; published in *Econometrica*, 37 (April, 1969), 171—92.

information-maximum likelihood (*FIML*). Three types of calculations have been made using the estimated system as a whole. All applications are non-stochastic in the sense that additive error terms are assumed to be zero in each estimated equation. Estimated coefficients are treated as though they are the correct values. For each period in the sample, dependent variables are estimated, given the observed independent variables and the lags. These are called *one-period simulations*. For each period in the sample, dependent variables are estimated 1929—41 and 1947—64 given the observed independent variables and the initial conditions, prior to 1929 and prior to 1947 respectively. These are called *multiperiod simulations*. Finally the dependent variables are estimated for the post-sample year 1965, given the 1965 observations on the independent variables and initial conditions prior to 1965. Summary measures of errors in *GNP* simulation and prediction are given in Table IV.

Table IV. Simulation and Prediction of Real *GNP* from Alternative Estimates (mean absolute percentage error)

	OLS	TSPC-4*	TSPC-8	FIML
One-period simulation	3.67	3.29	3.49	2.96
Multiperiod simulation	7.62	3.99	5.79	10.58
Ex-post prediction	1.56	1.52	1.62	0.95

*TSPC-6 is used for ex-post predictions.

Deeper study of all the variables and other performance aspects of the system are needed to draw strong conclusions

72

from this empirical study, but some basic principles are illustrated in this tabulation.

1. Best fitting individual equations do not necessarily constitute a best fitting system. Residual error is minimal, in the square, for *OLS*, but the performance of the *OLS* system is not superior. In particular, in long run simulations the *OLS* version runs far astray. This indicates that small amounts of *OLS* bias or inconsistency show up in error cumulation for multiperiod extrapolation.

2. In performing data-reduction on the set of independent variables for *TSLS* estimation, there appears to be a best number of principal components for purposes of simulation and prediction. There is a point in seeking best estimates for purposes of prediction. In more extensive testing of different estimates of this model, *TSPC*-4 performs best over a wide variety of tests.

3. The principle of maximum likelihood states that we have parameter estimates that maximize the probability of obtaining the observed sample of dependent variables, given the independent variables and the lagged variables. It is noteworthy that *FIML* performs well on one-period simulations and one-period ex-post prediction. This is what the principle states. It does not perform very well in multiperiod simulation. Lagged values are not treated as given in this kind of calculation.

It is not evident from the table but is a fact that *FIML* estimates give a poor cyclical picture of the Great Depression, in contrast with the other estimates, for multiperiod simulation, but they give a reasonable cyclical pattern for the Great Depression in one-period simulation.

Using single-equation methods of estimation, OLS or $TSPC$, it is possible to compute a system in which all coefficients appear to be plausible and especially of the correct sign. There is a sign deviate by the $FIML$ method and possibly some individual coefficients of dubious magnitude.

In this discussion of improvement of predictive ability, attention has been focused on the treatment of problems of lags and serial dependence. There is an equally large problem associated with the uncertainty of our knowledge about independent variables and possible ways of dealing with this form of uncertainty. Of course, one approach would be to enlarge our systems by explaining more of these variables in an endogenous way. In many cases, though, our knowledge about them is so limited that we may increase prediction error by using a poor explanation of their behavior. My preference is for presentation of multiple predictions according to alternative exogenous assumptions revealing the range of possibilities for the occurrence of exogenous events.

Point forecasts obscure the nature of the error associated with imperfect knowledge of the coefficients of a model and the variability of the disturbances. Methods of allowing for standard error of forecast are well understood, although the actual calculation of such standard errors has yet to be done for large, complicated systems. The uncertainty associated with imperfect knowledge of exogenous variables or parametric changes is not included in standard error formulas. Given our lack of knowledge about political actions, decisions of power groups in the society, and similar external variations, my preference is to provide a range of predictions, each associated with plausible values of exogenous variables covering likely contingencies. In this form, predictions are most useful to policy makers who have to act on the basis of ex-ante forecasts.

74

GENERALIZED MULTIPLIER ANALYSIS

In previous days, before the regular use of computers to solve and simulate large scale models, the effects of alternative conditions or values of exogenous variables were studied by using the multipliers of a system. These reduced form parameters show the response of dependent variables to changes in independent variables or parameters. They are typified by the well-known concept of the Keynesian multiplier, showing the ratio of the change in national income or product associated with a change in the exogenous component of investment. Similar multipliers were used for changes in government spending, taxes, transfer payments, and exports. Using approximate multipliers we were able to predict the effects of fiscal policy or deviations from any basic prediction path.

In the linear system

$$y_t = - A_o^{-1} \sum_{i=1}^{p} A_i y_{t-i} - A_o^{-1} B x_t + A_o^{-1} e_t,$$

impact multipliers, realized in the first period of a changed situation, would be evaluated from elements of $- A_o^{-1} B$, The typical expression is

$$\frac{\partial y_{it}}{\partial x_{jt}} = - \sum_{k=1}^{n} a_o^{ik} \beta_{kj} .$$

The i-th row of $- A_o^{-1}$ contains $- a_o^{ik}$ $(k = 1, 2, \ldots, n)$ and the j-th column of B contains β_{kj} $(k = 1, 2, \ldots, n)$. The estimated values of a_o^{ik} and β_{kj}, when inserted in this formula, give estimated values of the multiplier expression.

75

There are three limitations to the generality of this expression: 1. It is a static value *at impact* and does not show the cumulated multiplier effect if the change in the exogenous variable is sustained over many periods. 2. It assumes that only one element of x_t is being changed. 3. It refers in this closed mathematical form to a linear system. I want to generalize the multiplier concept to cover evaluations of dynamic multipliers, from nonlinear systems, with more general forms of change. A dynamic multiplier cumulates effects of change over many time periods. This can be done in linear dynamic systems, beyond the impact effects evaluated above, but the expressions become somewhat more complicated.[1] A more serious problem is to show, in simple formulas, the effects of more realistic combined changes. Several elements of x_t may change simultaneously; some parameter values may also be changed; some changes may be sustained while others are temporary. It is awkward to derive one single formula to cover these more complicated »packages» of change. Finally, general expressions for change in a nonlinear system do not exist in parametric form as in a linear system. For these reasons, it is not practical to try to handle all relevant problems of prediction by multiplier analysis. A limited number of deviants from the standard forecast can be made with simple multiplier calculations, but the generalization of the whole multiplier concept being considered here is actually a problem in the generation of alternative predictions. The making of predictions and the generalization of the multiplier concept are, as I see it, simply different facets of the same technique.

1. See A. S. Goldberger, Econometric Theory, (N.Y.: John Wiley and Sons, 1964), pp. 374—76.

The generalized multiplier is obtained by first computing a »control» solution. This is the same thing as the computation of the standard prediction. Let us label this solution as $y^c_{i,\,T+1}$, $y^c_{i,\,T+2}, \ldots, y^c_{i,\,T+F}$. This calculation can be ex-ante or ex-post, within or outside the sample. The next step is the preparation of a »deviant» solution labeled $y^d_{i,\,T+1}, y^d_{i,\,T+2}, \ldots, y^d_{i,\,T+F}$. This corresponds to any set of prescribed changes in the control solution. The time paths of elements of x_t can be altered in any way over the time range $t = T + 1, T + 2, \ldots, T + F$. Parameter values can similarly be changed. The comparison of the two time paths

$$y^c_{i,\,T+1}, y^c_{i,\,T+2}, \ldots, y^c_{i,\,T+F}$$

and

$$y^d_{i,\,T+1}, y^d_{i,\,T+2}, \ldots, y^d_{i,\,T+F}$$

replace the old concept of the static multiplier for linear systems. If the change in x_t is a simple change in a single element

$$\Delta = x^d_{i,\,T+j} - x^c_{i,\,T+j}$$

then the dynamic multiplier for the j-th period is

$$\frac{y^d_{i,\,T+j} - y^c_{i,\,T+j}}{\Delta}.$$

Since our computer methods for solving (approximately) large nonlinear dynamic systems are so fast, it is quick and easy to evaluate both the control solution and many deviants. There is no need any longer to guess at $y^d_{i,\,t+j}$ through some rough multiplier calculations; we can readily evaluate this variable directly and from such calculations build up an inventory of typical multiplier values (nonlinear and dynamic).

Thus, we see that the process of presenting alternative predictions corresponding to alternative assumptions about independent variables, whether because of uncertainty or curiosity about policy effects, is really an application of generalized multiplier analysis. Modern computer methods for system solution make these approaches the same and make it possible for us to present ranges of predictions associated with ranges of contingent events or policies as a standard form of prediction.

THE DEGREE OF AGGREGATION

The current tendency in macroeconometric model building is distinctly toward the development of larger systems. Some of the earlier models were strongly aggregated by economic sector, as well as by calendar time. The models currently being used in short run quarterly forecasts are larger than their predecessors. The Wharton-EFU Model has 47 stochastic equations and 29 identities. It has two major endogenous sectors—manufacturing and nonmanufacturing. It is commonplace to work with models of this size. Technically it is feasible from the view points of data preparation, computation for estimation, computation for solution, up-dating, and quick application. Larger models of 300 equations, such as the Brookings Model, are feasible but somewhat less easy to build and manipulate.

The reason why model building has gone in the direction of bigness (disaggregation by sector) is clear. Bigger models treat more economic detail, with finer grained structural equations, and they should be capable of accomplishing more. This argument sounds very well in principle, but it may not work out that way. Data for bigger models may be poor, and our ability

78

to comprehend bigger models may be deficient. These facts may lead to poorer results from big systems. The over riding need, however, to build large systems rests on the demands of users. Private companies, government agencies, and international bodies want to know much more than estimates of future *GNP* totals. At a minimum, they want predictions of price level, wage rate, employment, profits, interest rate and many other major aggregates. In addition, there is an insatiable request for predictions of activity in specific industries and specific markets. Users of economic predictions want and need simultaneous predictions for a large number of variables. The natural way to meet this request appears to be to build larger and larger econometric models, commensurate with our ability to manage such large systems. The models of the future are bound to be large systems, approaching as many as 1000 equations in size, and disaggregating in time to reach monthly movements. There will be degrees-of-freedom problems in constructing such systems, but such obstacles are not insurmountable. Estimation with data reduction techniques (principal components used with *TSLS* and other methods) are feasible, and it is wrong to look simply at a comparison between the number of equations or parameters and the number of data points. With each data point, there are as many random variables as there are stochastic equations in the system. This adds to the overall initial number of degrees of freedom, although there are other limitational factors in deriving estimates. Once a system is estimated, there is no degree-of-freedom issue in applying it to problems of predictions except insofar as the number of degrees of freedom affect the sampling errors of the estimated coefficients.

It is well known that error cancellation occurs in aggregation or averaging. It is, therefore, alleged that aggregative relationships tend to be stable and even that a strongly aggregative

79

model may be a superior predictive device.[1] If attention is centered on pure *GNP* forecasting, then simple *GNP* models of no more than 4—6 relationships, are claimed to give very good predictions and probably better than those obtained from more sophisticated models. A simple *GNP* model is nearly in the class of naive models. It has the obvious limitation that it provides little information. A four-equation model predicts just four variables, and this is surely an inadequate objective for most decision makers.

The small model has the advantage that it is easy to deal with. It is easy to estimate, to solve, and to understand. It can be applied repeatedly, with little effort. But it has a serious analytical drawback in the context of the modern industrial economy. A model of this extremely limited size cannot always be adapted to large environmental changes. Tax law changes, big shifts in monetary policy, large changes in the international economy cannot be readily reflected in small systems. To reflect such events adequately would require a larger model — one that would no longer qualify as a small model. A certain critical size must be reached in order to accomodate taxes, transfers, price level, wage rate, interest rate, foreign trade, and all the main components of *GNP*. For prediction in the modern economy, models must have at least 15—20 stochastic relationships, but systems of 40—50 equations are to be distinctly preferred. There is no question about our being able to cope with such systems with today's facilities.

1. Irwin Friend and R. C. Jones, »Short Run Forecasting Models Incorporating Anticipatory Data», *Models of Income Determination, Studies in Income and Wealth*, Vol. 28, (Princeton: Princeton University Press, 1964).

Irwin Friend and Paul Taubman, »A Short Term Forecasting Model», The *Review of Economics and Statistics*, XLIV (August, 1964), 229—36.

It is possible to go in the direction of extreme disaggregation without being involved in the construction of mammoth systems. One of the next versions of the Brookings Model will contain separate equations for as many as 35 different industrial sectors and this will require the construction of a system of approximately 1000 equations. This is experimental and requires much research analysis. I have in mind the possibility of getting the same refined industry information for selected industries without becoming involved in the construction of 1000-equation systems.

One procedure would be to construct separate industrial *satellite* models to be grafted to single *master* macro models. A satellite model for industry i will consist of equations that jointly relate several sector variables and macro variables. The latter will be GNP, personal income, general price level, average interest rate, average wage rate and similar national economy variables.

$$f_{ij}\left(y_{i1t}, \ldots, y_{int}, x_{i1t}, \ldots, x_{imt}, z_{1t}, \ldots, z_{kt}\right) = e_{ijt}$$
$$j = 1, 2, \ldots, n$$

In the i-th industry, we have n equations relating n dependent industry variables (y_{ijt}), m independent industry variables (x_{ijt}), and k national macro variables, (z_{jt}). Lags in all these will be introduced in any given study. For parameter estimation, we may replace z_{jt} by $\hat{z}_{jt}$, values computed from the master model over the sample period. These will be ex-post simulated predictions. Such variables may be treated as exogenous variables in statistical estimation.

For purposes of prediction, we may use predictions of macro variables $z^f_{j, T+e}$, together with assumed values of industry independent variables, to obtain sector predictions. The macro variable predictions are obtained by solving the master model in a regular forecast situation.

81

Inter-relationships among the i-th sector variables can be studied in great detail in this way. A model that is comparable in size to the macro master model can be constructed and then grafted to the overall performance of the economy. The chain of causation is unidirectional from the master to the satellite model and not vice versa. This line of research has already been implemented in model studies of the automobile, steel, and agricultural sectors of the U.S. economy.* It is also being done for regional model building and prediction in the U.S. economy. † A further subdivision can be carried to the level of the individual firm. Given a prediction for the national economy from a master model, we can derive a prediction of an industry from a satellite model. Given the prediction of the satellite model, we can derive a prediction of an individual firm by establishing a relationship between that firm's market performance and its industry's activity. With our present state of knowledge and data availability, this seems to be an efficient and practical way to make microeconomic predictions.

In a model as large and detailed as the Brookings Model it has been found possible to make predictions (ex-post) for eight separate industrial sectors — 1. agriculture, 2. durable manufacturing, 3. nondurable manufacturing, 4. wholesale and retail trade, 5. regulated industry, 6. construction, 7. government enterprise, 8. »residual» industry. This has been implemented through a combination of input-output and final-demand analysis. Some of the same methods can be used to construct industrial sector predictions for a smaller model than the 300-equation Brookings Model. The basic input-output relationship used is

$$(I - A)\, y_t = f_t,$$

where y_t is an n-element vector of industry gross outputs and

f_t is an n-element vector of final demands. The well-known input-output matrix is written as $I—A$. Data are available on value-added $(V.A.)$ or GNP originating by industrial sector. With mark-up coefficients m_i, we can derive the approximate relationships.

$$m_i \, (V.A.)_{it} = y_{it} \, .$$

Approximation is involved because the mark-up coefficients are not constant. They can be varied along known trend or cyclical functions. Constructed time-series of f_t can be obtained from $(I — A) \, y_t$. This step is necessary because f_t is available only at selected dates.

Final demand functions are empirical relationships between elements of f_t and GNP components. We retain model consistency and determinacy by restricting the choice of GNP components $(gnp)_{it}$ to be those contained in the entire model as explicit endogenous variables and by imposing the restriction

$$\sum_{i=1}^{n} f_{it} + R_t = (GNP)_t$$

on the functions

$$f_{it} = g_i \left[(gnp)_{1t}, \ldots, (gnp)_{rt} \right].$$

The variable R_t is a reconciling item to account for the fact that final demand may not be defined precisely to add to GNP. The main issue in this reconciliation is the treatment of imports in final demand. Some imports may be allocated, together with comparable domestic production, as intermediate inputs into various sectors of the main body of the input-output table;

83

other imports could be treated as negative final demand or in a separate row of allocation of production costs. The determination of R_t is a highly technical matter, which should not deter us from considering the basic overall identity between the sum of final demands and total *GNP*. Coefficients of the empirical final demand equation can be estimated so as to preserve the final demand identity, or we may adopt a looser formulation, ignore the identity, add lag variables, price ratios and other model variables so as to improve the goodness of fit of the g_i-functions. If we follow this loose, empirical approach, we should take care that the discrepancy in the computed final demand identity is not large or growing. This would be especially important in long term prediction.

The input-output equations and the final demand equations are essential endogenous ingredients of the Brookings Model. We cannot obtain a complete system solution without using them, and we cannot obtain a solution for major parts, say, the *GNP* components, without using them.

A different use is made of

$$(I - A) y_t = f_t$$

$$f_{it} = g_i \left[(gnp)_{1t}, \ldots, (gnp)_{rt} \right]$$

in supplementary solutions of the Wharton-EFU Model. First the macro model is used for prediction of *GNP* and its components, $(gnp)_{it}$. Having these and estimates of the g_i-function, we predict f_{it} and substitute in the input-output equations to obtain y_t, using the 1958 table for $I - A$. These calculations are all made on the basis of the same 8-sector industry disaggregation used in the Brookings Model. A further consistency check is made by predicting value added for each sector from

$$m_i(V.A.)^f_{it} = y^f_{it}.$$

and evaluating the discrepancy

$$\sum_{i=1}^{n} (V.A.)^f_{it} - (GNP)^f_t = \delta^f_t.$$

The residual δ^f_t is allocated among sectors according to some arbitrary rule such as proportionality to the i-th sector's share in aggregate value added. In constrast with the role of the input-output system and the solutions for sector output in the Brookings Model solutions, the values of $(V.A.)^f_{it}$ obtained from the Wharton-EFU Model have no influence on the GNP solutions. We merely have a device for subdividing GNP predictions into separate industry predictions.

Experimental calculations with ex-post prediction simulations of the Brookings Model and both ex-ante and ex-post predictions of sectors based on the Wharton-EFU Model solutions have been made for the small scale of disaggregation by sectors listed above. It is unlikely that refined sectors at no more than the 2-digit manufacturing level could be predicted from relatively small systems. An adequate explanation of final demand in systems with 30 or more industrial sectors requires a very detailed decomposition of $(GNP)_t$ into components $(gnp)_{it}$. At a minimum, we shall need to expand the Wharton-EFU Model to more than 100 structural equations to accomodate this amount of detail, and the full integration of an input-output system of this size in the expansion of the Brookings Model will require something like 1000 equations.

Some experimental error calculations for seven industrial sectors based on Wharton-EFU ex-post predictions are shown in Table V.

85

Table V. Ex-post Prediction Error, One Quarter,
Gross Output of Seven Sectors, Wharton-EFU Model
(1953—1964, average absolute percentage error)

Sector	Error
Durable manufacturing	4.77
Nondurable manufacturing	1.45
Wholesale and retail trade	1.31
Regulated industries	1.62
Contract construction	4.33
Residual non farm industries	0.70
Farming	3.72

These are encouraging results, yet they leave room for
substantial improvement. All the errors are under 5 per cent,
but they are larger than corresponding errors of *GNP* components of the Model. Also, the largest error occurs in one of the
most important sectors, durable manufacturing. In these
calculations, there is no restriction imposed on the results that
the predicted total of gross output by sector be consistent with
predicted *GNP*. If this restriction is imposed, the percentage
error distribution is shifted towards more equality among
sectors, and there is distinct improvement in the accuracy of
prediction for durable manufacturing.

Another method of drawing on microeconomic data is to use
sample survey data elicited from individual respondents —
households and firms. These data are buying plans, advance
commitments, appraisals of individual financial condition, and
appraisals of market conditions. The most direct use of these
data would be the translation of intended purchase totals into
predicted purchases or the construction of indexes of purchasing
or sentiment as direct indicators of predicted actions. A more
analytical use would be in the form of realization equations

$$f_i(y_{1t}, \ldots, y_{nt}, y_{1, t-1}, \ldots, y_{n, t-p}, x_{1t}, \ldots, x_{mt}, A_{1t}, \ldots, A_{rt})$$

$$= e_{it}.$$

These equations are like our ordinary structural equations for a general nonlinear dynamic model, except that they contain indexes or value aggregates of microeconomic anticipations $A_{1t}, \ldots, A_{rt}$ in addition to the regular objective variables that we have been considering previously. The A_{it} are determined with some lead time from individual reports (questionnaires, interviews, official forms, etc.). They are treated as independent variables for the purpose of estimating the parameters of the functions, f_i. We can use the A_{it} in prediction by inserting their expected future values, ascertained in advance, together with values for x_{it} and $y_{i, t-j}$ in the estimated equation system and solve for y_{it}. This may be done partially in individual equations or simultaneously in complete models.

The Wharton-EFU Model is a two-track system. Some of the equations have alternate forms that include anticipatory variables in addition to the usual dependent and independent variables. They are equations for expenditures on consumer durables (Survey Research Center Index of Consumer Attitudes), expenditures on automobiles (Survey Research Center Index of Consumer Attitudes), manufacturing investment (OBE-SEC Investment Intentions), regulated industry investment (OBE-SEC Investment Intentions), residential housing expenditures (housing starts). These are very different kinds of anticipatory variables. Some are subjective attitudes, and some are commitments or physical acts. The latter may eventually be included as ordinary variables of an expanded system. The lead time of reports on the anticipatory variables is nearly two quarters; therefore we replace the standard versions of these equations and solve the model ahead for two quarters using the anticipatory variables. Thus two predictions are made quarterly — using and not using equations with anticipatory variables. In simulations over the sample period, ex-post predictions one and two quarters ahead are slightly better using the anticipations form of the equations instead of the purely objective forms.

Table VI. Ex-Post Predictions, Error of Selected Variables, Wharton-EFU Model, With and Without Anticipations, 1953—1964.

Variable	Period of prediction	Average absolute error	
		with anti-cipations	without anti-cipations
GNP, billions of 1958 dollars	1 quarter	4.10	5.47
	2 quarters	4.20	6.16
Consumer expenditures, billions	1 quarter	2.37	3.31
of current dollars	2 quarters	2.68	3.75
Manufacturing investment,	1 quarter	0.31	0.50
billions of 1958 dollars	2 quarters	0.49	0.95
Regulated industry investment,	1 quarter	0.43	0.44
billions of 1958 dollars	2 quarters	0.43	0.44
Residential construction, billions	1 quarter	0.35	0.86
of 1958 dollars	2 quarters	0.35	0.86
Unemployment rate, per cent	1 quarter	0.97	1.03
	2 quarters	0.87	1.00
GNP price deflator, index,	1 quarter	0.28	0.27
1958 base = 100	2 quarters	0.47	0.52

It is encouraging that the use of anticipatory variables may improve our very short run predictions, but these variables have limited use at present. We can predict ahead for periods in which they are known, as expected values, but we have not successfully generated anticipations endogenously on a widespread basis, and we are unable to make predictions one or two years ahead.[1] Progress will undoubtedly be made in developing more anticipatory series, in extending their time horizon, and in treating them endogenously. These microeconomic data have a definite contribution to make to prediction methods in the near future.

The use of anticipations variables in a model does not mean that I have succumbed to the notion that a forecasting model, as distinct from a structural model, has an independent existence. I regard the use of anticipations variables as the first, and necessary step, in constructing a complete structural model in which the effect of anticipations on observed behavior is estimated in step one *and* the explanation of anticipations in terms of ordinary objective economic variables is compeleted in step two. I do not think that we are yet ready for the second step although we have some results on that aspect. Experimentation with models in which only the first step is completed does not imply that we are constructing a forecasting model that lacks structural content.

OTHER METHODS OF PREDICTION

I have been treating the problem of prediction as though it is natural to consider it as an econometric problem based on a

---

1. Dale Jorgenson has attempted to explain both investment intentions and investment expenditures; see his chapter, »Anticipations and Investment Behavior», *Brookings Quarterly Econometric Model of the U.S.*, ed. J. Duesenberry, et.al. (Chicago: Rand McNally, 1965).

mathematical-statistical model. Part of the problem is in estimation of the model in a form that best serves a prediction objective, and part of the problem is in the use of a model in a particular way for prediction. In practice, I have argued that personal judgment and expert opinion cannot be neglected. The formal model should serve as a means to accomodate and interpret judgmental information for the purposes of prediction. Complete reliance on judgment and informed opinion could constitute an alternative approach to prediction, but I shall not consider this approach further because there is little of systematic methodology or analysis to be said. I have suggested, following Adams and Evans, that an average of judgmental forecasts can be used as a standard of reference with which to judge formal prediction methods, and I shall not dwell on the obvious in arguing for good judgment in developing good forecasts.

There are, however, other formal statistical methods of prediction that can be considered as alternatives to the econometric approach that I have been discussing. I shall concentrate on the *indicator* method developed by the National Bureau of Economic Research and some forms of pure time-series analysis such as autoregression and spectral analysis.

The indicator method is based on a definition of *the business cycle* and a chronology of *cyclical phases* and *turning points*.[1] *Reference cycle dates* are periods (defined at a particular month) at which the business cycles either reached a peak or a trough. These points date back to the middle of the 19th century. A large number of economic statistical series have been processed

1. See e.g. A. F. Burns and W. C. Mitchell, *Measuring Business Cycles*, (New York: National Bureau of Economic Research, 1946) and *Business Cycle Indicators*, ed. by G. H. Moore, 3 vols., (Princeton: Princeton Univ. Press, 1961).

(seasonally smoothed, e.g.) and studied as *specific cycles*. A subgroup of series has been selected from 500—1000 series as showing stable and persistent patterns of timing — either leading, coinciding with, or lagging the reference cycle. When leading series definitely show a cyclical turn, we may interpret this as a prediction of a future cyclical movement. It is confirmed when coincident series show the same turn. When lagging series finally turn, we can be assured that we have moved to the next phase of the cyclical process. Presumably these methods are applicable at either a downturn or an upturn.

The main relationships are those of timing. Some quantitative information is used although not necessarily in a formal way. When a large percentage of indicators *(diffusion indexes)* show a particular turn, one may feel very strong about that turn. When sensitive series turn by a large amount one may expect a severe turn. Principally, though, the information is indicative of direction of movement, only, and most useful at turning points of activity. Information is available up to the time of the latest reports, and predictive information extends in the future only by the amount of lead time. It is, therefore, not suitable for very long projections, and a disadvantage has been that we have not really known that a turn in activity has occurred until some months after the event. Reporting is always getting better, but even in the best of circumstances, the delays, when coupled with a lack of apparatus for projection ahead, dilute the use of the NBER methods as predictive devices. To give an example, I recall vividly that the downturn that occurred in the autumn of 1948 was not recognized as a clear turn in spring, 1949. It was still being debated at NBER in the spring whether the economy had actually turned down during the previous autumn. Of course, reporting methods are considerably improved today, but it is still difficult to date a turning point until

91

after the event has occurred. In autumn, 1967, we have been told that a downturn probably did not occur in the first quarter of 1967.

Another problem has been the emission of false signals. There are several occasions (spring 1956, summer 1962, winter 1967) when large numbers of leading indicators had turned down, yet the economy did not subsequently turn into recession. The false signals may come from many sources, but a notorious bad actor has been an index of stock market prices. Given the methodology of collecting the series that happen to be available and classifying them by lead-lag chronology, it is not difficult to see how a series like stock market prices can be included in the list of sensitive leading indicators. This series, however, may have little structural significance. It may simply be indicative of numerous other variables that have clearer economic meaning and ought not to be used in economic prediction. It is true that some econometric model builders have tried to introduce stock market prices as explanatory variables in some individual relationships, motivated by the high correlations found, and by a desire to reflect the cost of equity capital, but since no one has ever managed to »explain» stock market prices it seems to be of little use, especially in prediction.

In the leading group of series, we find duplication of information. Among available series, there are several that say something about employment conditions, several that say something about investment planning, several that say something about business formation, etc. There is duplication of effort; there is a failure to weed out what is structurally important from a point of view of economic analysis and a tendency to accept whatever happens to be available whether it is hours worked, help wanted advertising, or some other dimension of labor market conditions. There is a salutary effort now to group

92

more series by economic process or sector and not to rely so much on roughly duplicative series.[1]

Between the leading, coincident, and lagging group there is some economic rationale. Orders must come before expenditure; inventories must be slow in being depleted or built up; action should be taken on hours of work before it is taken on employment when conditions change. These are, however, loose formulations. The disadvantage of this looseness is that prediction in a broad sense cannot be made. There may be limited information for straightforward ex-ante prediction but not for conditional prediction. There is no formal framework to tell us what to expect if basic policy parameters change, if exogenous variables change, or if various hypothetical situations are assumed to occur. To predict in a broad sense, we need understanding and formal structure. The indicator method is relatively uninformative about understanding of structural characteristics. It definitely provides useful economic information, but it has serious limitations.

Each individual economic series in the NBER indicator collection is analyzed in terms of its own past history (specific cycle patterns) and in relation to the overall business cycle (reference cycle patterns). This is not the whole of their method because the lead-lag relationships establish, in a somewhat unstructured way, inter-relationships within the economy, but the essence of the approach is to study each series in terms of its own past history. A more formal time series analysis may accomplish similar ends.

1. J. Shishkin and G. H. Moore, »Composite Indexes of Leading, Coinciding and Lagging Indicators, 1948—67», supplement to *National Bureau Report 1*. (New York: National Bureau of Economic Research, 1968).

Autoregression is a convenient way of estimating behavior of any single variable in terms of its own past history.

$$y_t = \sum_{i=1}^{p} \varrho_i y_{t-i} + e_t.$$

For a given value of p, y_t may be regressed on its own lags. The value of p may be selected according to some empirical rule. Perhaps successive lags can be added to least squares regressions,

$$\sum_{t=1}^{T} e_t^2 = \text{min.},$$

as long as there is a statistically significant decrease in estimated residual variance. Successive values of y_{t-i} $(i = 1, 2, \ldots, p)$ may be highly intercorrelated, thus obscuring the statistical significance of separate coefficients, or a lag distribution can be used in order to reduce the number of parameters being estimated. There is, however, no accepted statistical criteria for deciding on the best value of p, with restrictions on various values of ϱ_i $(1 < i < p)$. It would be purely a matter of empirical search for »good» relationships with some a priori, but arbitrary, criteria of fit, or it may be estimation according to a fixed technique with arbitrary restrictions on p. Each of a number of variables to be predicted could be assumed to be generated by a second order or possibly a third order autoregressive process. The usual criterion would then be uniform regression calculations for each variable on its first, second, and third lags.

This is not unlike a naive model which predicts each variable from

94

$$y_t = y_{t-1} + e_t$$

or

$$y_t - y_{t-1} = y_{t-1} - y_{t-2} + e_t.$$

The principal difference is that the more general autoregression

$$y_t = \varrho_1 y_{t-1} + \varrho_2 y_{t-2} + e_t$$

allows the unknown parameters ϱ_1 and ϱ_2 to be estimated from sample data on y_t; whereas the other naive models have a priori coefficients. The pure autoregressive approach to forecasting is a »quasi naive» model; it is automatic and simple, but it involves some theory. Orcutt attempted to provide such a theory by making statistical tests of the hypothesis that each of Tinbergen's endogenous variables could have been drawn from a common autoregressive process, with different random errors for each variable.[1] In this case, one forecast formula could be used for each different variable. In a more empirical approach without such a theoretical derivation or justification there can be as many estimated autoregressions as there are variables.

It is not necessary to be restricted to regression of a variable on its own lags; there can be cross lags as well, but this becomes complicated at a rapid rate if many variables are being predicted at once.

$$y_{it} = \sum_{k=1}^{p} \sum_{j=1}^{n} \varrho_{ijk} y_{j,\ t-k} + e_{it}.$$

By using lags across variables we add to the complexity of the process and will probably, in any practical case, have to restrict the legth of lag considered.

1. G. H. Orcutt, *op.cit.*

The system of equations with cross lags has the simplification of being in reduced form with only lagged variables on the right hand side; otherwise it is very much like a part of a structural model, namely a part that neglects the effects of exogenous variables. That is a significant defect of pure time series analysis, either in autoregressive form or in the form of NBER cyclical analysis. There is direct consideration only of the effects of history of endogenous variables and a disregard, in prediction, of current effects of exogenous variables. Government fiscal variables, overseas variables, monetary control variables, and natural forces are likely to be big. They are certainly as important for the economy as historical values of endogenous variables. Any forecasting system that neglects their current and extrapolated influence is bound to miss many of the important turns of economic life. Naive models are likely to perform worst; quasi-naive models will do somewhat better because they are guided by parameter estimates that have sample content; finally we have structural models that combine lags (as in naive and quasi-naive models), parameter estimates based on sample experience (as in quasi-naive models), exogenous variables, a priori expert judgment, a priori economic analysis, and knowledge about structural parameters.

Pure time series analysis with formal mathematical structure need not necessarily be of an autoregressive type. We could fit equations of the form

$$y_t = f(t) + e_t,$$

where $f(t)$ is some parametric function of time. It could be a polynomial in t, trigonometric function, or the solution form of linear difference equations. These do not seem to be especially promising. Predictions of *cyclical behavior* can be made however

96

through the methods of stochastic simulation or spectral analysis. These are preferred alternatives to fitting

$$y_t = f(t) + e_t$$

in trigonometric form or in solution form associated with linear difference equations. The objective of cyclical analysis is not to predict future levels of variables at particular time points but to estimate the frequency, amplitude, and phase characteristics of future fluctuations. It represents an attempt to say whether cyclical fluctuations are expected to occur in the future and what the characteristics of these fluctuations are likely to be. This form of analysis will, however, require knowledge of the structural estimates of the original system.

Consider the estimated linear equation system

$$\sum_{i=0}^{p} \hat{A}_i y_{t-i} + \hat{B} x_t = 0.$$

For a hypothetical future period $t = T + 1, \ldots, T + F$ the vector x_t is assigned values $x_{T+1}, \ldots, x_{T+F}$. These may follow any a priori path, but an eminently reasonable one would be the extrapolation of historical trends in the components of x_t. For the future period, instead of fixing the errors at mean values

$$e_{T+1} = \ldots = e_{T+F} = 0,$$

errors can be drawn from random number generators with estimated probability characteristics. The usual practice is to assume that $e_{T+1}, \ldots, e_{T+F}$ are multivariate normal with covariance matrix Σ. The latter is the sample estimate.

The Adelman—Adelman stochastic simulation of the estimated Klein—Goldberger model over a hypothetical stretch of 100 years provides a prediction of the occurrence of business cycles in the future with 4-year periodicity, moderate amplitude, and a number of numerical cyclical characteristics — the mean length of upswing, the mean length of downswing, the percentage of leading series, the percentage of lagging series, etc.[1] The form of the model they used was not entirely linear, but it approximately followed the described procedure.

By using spectral analysis, E. P. Howrey reached similar conclusions with the same model.[2] This may be interpreted as *infinite* stochastic simulation. The spectrum representation of the disturbance process v_t is

$$v_t = \int_{-\pi}^{\pi} e^{i\omega t}\, d V\,(\omega),$$

where

$$d V(\omega) = \frac{1}{2\pi} \sum_{s=-\infty}^{\infty} e^{-i\omega s}\, v_s.$$

The spectrum matrix of the disturbance process is

$$f(\omega) = E[d V\,(\omega)\, d V^*\,(\omega)] = \frac{1}{2\pi} \sum_{s=-\infty}^{\infty} e^{-i\omega s}\, E[v_t\, v_{t-s}^*].$$

* represents the conjugate transpose operation.

The *final form* relationship between the endogenous variables of a system and the error terms enables us to transform the spectrum matrix of the disturbance process into the spectrum matrix of the endogenous process of the system. Since

1. I. and F. L. Adelman, »The Dynamic Properties of the Klein—Goldberger Model», *Econometrica*, 27 (October, 1959), 596—625.
2. E. P. Howrey, »Stochastic Properties of the Klein—Goldberger Model», Econometric Research Program, Princeton University, 1967, (unpublished).

$$y_t = -\frac{a(L)}{\varDelta(L)} B \, x_t + \frac{a(L)}{\varDelta(L)} \, v_t,$$

we have

$$\frac{a(L)}{\varDelta(L)} \int_{-\pi}^{\pi} e^{i\omega t} \, dV(\omega) = \int_{-\pi}^{\pi} e^{i\omega t} \, T(\omega) \, dV(\omega),$$

and the spectrum matrix of the system is

$$F(\omega) = E[T(\omega) \, dV(\omega) \, dV^*(\omega) \, T^*(\omega)]$$

$$= T(\omega) f(\omega) \, T^*(\omega).$$

$F(\omega)$ is thus a transformation of $f(\omega)$, using the transfer matrix $T(\omega)$.

Howrey's calculations with a linearized version of the Klein—Goldberger model in the endogenous tax case, show cycle length of 4—5 years and phase relationships among various series that correspond to those found by NBER methods. This exercise simply confirms the predictive results of the Adelman—Adelman type of simulation by solving the model forward into the indefinite future.*

PREDICTIVE VS. STRUCTURAL MODELS

For some time, I have maintained the position that there is no point in trying to construct models that are purely of use in prediction and deny that such models have an existence of their own apart from structural models. I would repeat earlier assertions that best predictions will be made from best structural models.

There is no single best model. Alternative models will always exist according to the degree of disaggregation that we desire to achieve. But even for a given degree of disaggregation, there is not enough sharpness in economic data to lead us to the clear cut choice of one single model as better than other plausible ones. It is, however, an achievement to find a single model that consistently performs well and is firmly based on a priori information.

Whether our objectives are minimal prediction error or best estimate of parameters we shall always need estimates of the detailed structure. This does not mean that there is necessarily a best single set of parameter estimates; alternative estimation methods can be used for alternative purposes, but it does mean that we should always be trying to estimate the underlying structure and should not try to estimate reduced forms, final forms, or solution forms without the underlying structure. It also means that we should not try to estimate pure empirical regularities without specifying a structure that could have generated these regularities.

In the pure time series analysis of unstructured autoregression or indicator analysis, there is not necessarily an attempt to specify an underlying structure, and these techniques are consequently not useful in conditional prediction. They ought to reveal defects in repeated trials of unconditional prediction. On the other hand, numerical simulation and spectral analysis of a model, are time series methods that do depend on structural information. In this form, time series analysis can be used for prediction on a structural basis.

It is difficult to know in advance of statistical research exactly what uses an estimated model is to be put to. It may be wanted for straightforward prediction, occasionally for the period immediately ahead and occasionally for an intermediate period a few years ahead. I am ruling out long range prediction of decades or more as not being within our grasp, at the moment, on the same scientific basis as short run prediction. Alternatively, an estimated model may be wanted for ex-post simulation to re-create history, for stochastic simulation, for various forms of conditional policy prediction, for testing economic theory, for demonstrating cyclical characteristics, etc.[1] Generally, we want a versatile model that is capable of serving many ends. There is still a fair amount of overhead research assistance and computation time involved with each model project; therefore it is not feasible to think of constructing a separate model for each individual objective. A versatile model must be a structural model because many applications will require detailed knowledge of structural composition. It means that we may want to split sample estimation and model application into two separate statistical steps instead of treating the problem as one large step in statistical inference.[2] Robust methods of parameter estimation in the sample period will be wanted to provide a base for a wide variety of applications of the estimated model outside the sample period.

In making this plea for structural analysis even if objectives center around forecasting applications, have I neglected to consider sufficiently sophisticated methods of pure time series analysis? I feel confident on the basis of repeated applications of the Wharton-EFU Model to a wide variety of forecasting problems for five years that the use of an estimated structural model

1. The study of alternative policies from conditional predictions is probably the most important single application of estimated models.

2. The one-step procedure is outlined in T. Haavelmo, *The Probability Approach in Econometrics*, supplement to *Econometrica*, 12 (July, 1944) esp. ch. VI.

is clearly superior to any pure time series analysis that has no explicit theory of behavior built into it. It has, on occasion, been suggested that pure prediction schemes be carried out on a »juggernaut» basis. In the autoregressive equation

$$y_t = \sum_{i=1}^{p} \varrho_i y_{t-i} + e_t$$

we could let p be some number such as 300 (months or quarters, possibly). A few economic series could be reconstructed for spans of more than 100 years, and large scale computers can handle estimation problems of great size. Let us suppose that very high autoregression or very long expressions in Fourier Series can be fit to historical data. Will this approach improve our ability to predict? It has never been done, but there is little in the way of scientific hunches to suggest that more of the past will help us foresee more of the future. The economy has changed in the direction of becoming more dependent on what we now call exogenous variables. Without knowledge of these and the way they affect the economy, my guess is that the »juggernaut» approach will not improve our predictive ability. Another dimension to the »juggernaut» approach is to establish a multitude of reporting stations and observers throughout strategic areas of the economy. More and quicker reports on leading indicators; weekly estimates of GNP; the development of new series; and similar data collection activities would certainly provide useful information. Again since this approach has not been followed on a massive scale, we cannot really say whether the new information gathered could be digested and used wisely to improve economic prediction. Without being used to construct models of behavior with structural parameter estimation, I fail to see how such masses of information could

102

be used to make conditional prediction. I think that unconditional prediction will also need to have such new data digested and used to build structural models. This is a research hunch and not an established finding. We can always use more information, more skilled manpower, and more sophisticated hardware, but I feel that economic prediction will be able to improve through the use of these resources only if they are directed into econometric model building efforts that give us understanding into the ways of functioning of the economy.

NOTES TO THE ORIGINAL EDITION

P. 22, * D.W. Katzner and L.R. Klein, "On the Possibility of the General Linear Economic Model", *Economic Models, Estimation, and Risk Programming*, ed. by K.A. Fox et. al., (Berlin: Springer-Verlag, 1969).

P. 38, Note 1, * A paper entitled "Estimation of Forecast Error in a Dynamic and/or Non-Linear Econometric Model" was presented to the Evanston meeting of the Econometric Society, December, 1968.

P. 44, * Updated Wharton Model errors for 1968 and 1969 are −13 and −12, respectively. Even with these two unusually poor performances, the average absolute error of the Wharton Model is less than $6.0 billion. The 1968 error is inflated by the delay in the passage of the tax surcharge. A conditional forecast that assumed no surcharge is in error by only $4.0 billion. The corresponding errors in the Federal Reserve Tabulation are −16 and −12, respectively.

The Wharton Model performed up to its usual standard in predicting real GNP for 1968 and 1969; the errors were in misjudgment of the degree of price inflation. The 1968 and 1969 errors in real GNP (1958 dollars) are −3.2 and +3.6, respectively.

P. 46, Note 1, * A detailed study of various ex post and ex ante forecasts with the Wharton Model is contained in the paper by M.K. Evans,

Y.Haitovsky, and G.I. Treyz, "An Analysis of Forecasting Properties of U.S. Econometric Models," Conference on Research in Income and Wealth, Cambridge, Massachusetts, November, 1969.

P. 57, Note 1, * The asymptotic bias of α obtained by minimizing the squared error over the solution path of the autoregressive equation in the sample period has been found to be directly proportional to σ_e^2 and inversely proportional to y_0. This result is due to Michael Hartley, formerly of the Wharton Econometric Forecasting Unit.

P. 82, * See *Essays in Industrial Econometrics*, I and II, ed. by L.R. Klein, (Philadelphia: Wharton School of Finance and Commerce, University of Pennsylvania, 1969).

† R. Crow, *An Econometric Model of the Northeast Corridor of the United States*, and N. Glickman, *An Econometric Model of the Philadelphia Region*, Ph.D. dissertations, University of Pennsylvania, 1969.

P. 99, * Stochastic simulations of the Wharton and the Office of Business Economics (U.S. Department of Commerce) quarterly models have been analyzed by spectral methods for their cyclical implications in papers prepared by M.K. Evans, L.R. Klein and M.Saito, and G. Green, respectively, for the Conference on Research in Income and Wealth, Cambridge, Massachusetts, November, 1969. These new studies generalize the Adelman and Adelman study of the Klein-Goldberger Model by drawing random errors so as to preserve the entire unlagged and serial covariance structure of the sample estimates of residuals in stochastic equations and by replicating the simulations many times. The spectral analysis of the simulations generalize Howrey's technique by avoiding the necessity to make linear approximations to the structural equations.

There is good evidence of the existence of a four year (16 quarter) cycle in the stochastic simulations with serially correlated random errors.

APPENDIX

In the Essay I have discussed in general terms the methods to be used in economic prediction. Here I place the discussion in a practical setting of actual forecasting.

A. THE MAKING OF A FORECAST

1. The format

Economic prediction is not uniperiod, unidimensional, or mechanical. It is a mixture of art and science, of formula and judgment, of statistical and nonstatistical information. There should be no single forecast for a future stretch of time. Over a period of seven years, the Wharton Econometric Forecasting Unit of the University of Pennsylvania has developed an approach to economic prediction that will be explained in this appendix, as an implementation of many of the ideas contained in this Essay.

Every quarter, academic econometricians meet with professional economists from major U.S. corporations and public institutions to develop an econometric forecast by quarters over a time horizon of eight quarters. At the time of meeting, the current quarter is one month old, and the first "prediction" quarter is this current quarter. Its economic results are not yet known in terms of statistical performance, but the investigator cannot be unaware of life that is taking place around him. Seven additional quarters are forecast. These are genuine extrapolations into the future.

Just after the middle of January, April, July, and October, the main economic data of the preceding quarter become available in the United States. These are principally the component series of the national income and product accounts, but they also consist of price, employment, and financial statistics. Prior to the first day of February, May, August, and November estimates are available for all variables of the Wharton–EFU Model for the just-completed quarter and all previous quarters needed for lagged variables. The

105

series in the Model data bank are updated, and the computer solution program for the equation system is executed with new revised lags and with assumptions for the exogenous variables, tax parameters, monetary control parameters, etc. These are trial prediction series.

The preliminary forecasts are usually available by the first day of the second month of each quarter. Different forecasts are made according to the uncertainties surrounding various combinations of exogenous variables or controlled parameters. That is to say, future policies or contingent events are never known with certainty, and several alternative solutions are prepared, at all stages, to cover the likely cases. There are usually between two and five alternatives.

As the Model estimates are not revised more than once in every two or three years, there are often substantial data revisions that lead to significant discrepancies between the data base for the coefficients of the equation system and the data base for the prediction exercise. In terms of the updated, revised series, therefore, the residuals for each structural equation of the Model are computed for the past six quarters to detect data biases or possible changes in behavior patterns. Some residuals are known to be freakish and temporary.[1] Some are associated with major disturbances such as a military confrontation (Korea, Vietnam), an international crisis (Suez Canal closing), a strike (1959 steel strike, 1969 dock strike, 1964 General Motors strike), or introduction of new economic devices (Euro dollar balances, certificates of deposit).

Each residual is examined for its explanation in terms of data revision, freak event, sustained disturbance, new devices, etc. To the equations of the model, additive constants are appended to put the system "on track" for the just-completed quarter. These "constant adjustments" are then programmed for future quarters or dropped if they are known to be temporary phenomena.

The adjusted equation system then provides forecast scenarios for each package of exogenous assumptions. A meeting of academic econometricians and company or institutional economists is then

---

[1]The inventory accumulation of $20 billion in the fourth quarter of 1966 obviously generates residuals in inventory behavior that are not sustainable for future quarters.

called, a week later, to study the forecasts. The preliminary forecasts are examined in detail for plausibility of assumptions, reasonableness of "constant adjustments", conformity to last-minute information, and conformity to "inside" information. A consensus is reached at the forecast meeting on all inputs for the control solution and for plausible or interesting alternatives.

2. The roles of judgment and formal models

Various mechanical schemes have been studied to see, in retrospect, what the forecasting record would have been if adjustments to equation estimates had been used for extrapolation. The possible mechanical schemes are:

a. Error terms set equal to zero (deterministic case).
b. Errors fixed at nonzero average of most recent values (up to past six values).
c. Structural error terms in forecast period assumed to follow the autoregressive process that is estimated from sample residuals. Initial conditions for solution of these numerical autoregressive equations are last observations of residuals before sample period.
d. Mixtures of (a), (b), and (c). The autoregressive correction appears to improve extrapolations for first two or more periods and then to deteriorate. This suggests (c) for the first two periods and (a) for late periods.

No sustained improvement, beyond two or three quarters, has been found from analysis of existing fitted models. But ex-ante forecasts, using nonstatistical a priori information on the residuals in place of an autoregressive adjustment equation or other mechanical corrections, appear to give much lower prediction errors. Judgment and informed observation of the economic world is not enough by itself to make such good forecasts. On the other hand mechanical use of models, in construction and in application, does not seem to work well. It is the combination of the two approaches that produces the best results. The numerically estimated model provides a systematic and consistent device to filter or interpret a priori information in making economic forecasts. This is the method that has been used for many years with the Wharton–EFU Model.

107

Table A.I. Preliminary Forecasts, August 1, 1969
Summary

		1969.2	1969.3	1969.4	1970.1	1970.2	1970.3	1970.4	1971.1	1971.2
Consumer expenditures	(i)	570.7	580.5	588.3	598.8	607.5	619.2	628.3	636.4	645.4
	(ii)	570.7	587.2	597.1	605.8	614.3	622.0	630.1	637.9	646.5
	(iii)	570.7	586.0	594.4	601.3	608.1	615.6	624.3	632.7	641.8
	(iv)	570.7	580.5	588.3	602.3	611.8	620.1	628.2	635.8	644.6
Fixed capital formation	(i)	98.5	99.4	97.6	95.5	95.3	94.5	94.4	93.8	94.0
	(ii)	98.5	99.8	100.4	99.0	97.8	96.2	94.4	92.8	92.2
	(iii)	98.5	99.7	99.8	97.6	95.7	93.8	92.4	91.4	91.5
	(iv)	98.5	99.4	97.6	95.7	96.4	95.3	93.7	92.3	91.9
Residential construction (nonfarm)	(i)	31.9	30.8	30.7	30.5	31.0	32.3	33.8	34.5	34.3
	(ii)	31.9	31.4	31.5	30.8	30.6	30.8	31.5	31.8	31.8
	(iii)	31.9	31.3	31.2	30.4	30.3	30.9	32.3	33.7	34.3
	(iv)	31.9	30.9	30.7	30.8	31.3	32.0	32.4	32.4	32.1
Inventory investment	(i)	9.5	7.6	4.0	2.7	2.4	2.8	3.8	4.6	5.3
	(ii)	9.5	8.8	6.4	4.4	2.7	1.7	1.8	2.5	3.5
	(iii)	9.5	8.9	4.8	1.5	-0.5	-1.3	-0.1	1.6	3.5
	(iv)	9.5	7.6	4.0	3.3	3.5	3.3	3.2	3.4	4.0
Net exports	(i)	2.0	2.3	2.7	3.4	3.5	4.2	4.3	4.8	5.0
	(ii)	2.0	2.1	2.4	3.2	3.2	3.9	4.0	4.6	4.9

(iii)	2.0	2.1	2.5	3.4	3.6	4.4	4.6	5.2	5.5
(iv)	2.0	2.3	2.7	3.3	3.4	4.1	4.3	4.8	5.0
Government expenditures (i)	212.5	217.3	222.2	226.1	230.1	234.2	238.5	242.9	247.4
(ii)	212.5	217.3	222.2	226.1	230.1	234.2	238.5	242.9	247.4
(iii)	212.5	214.4	217.8	220.2	222.7	226.7	230.9	235.3	239.7
(iv)	212.5	217.3	222.2	226.1	230.1	234.2	238.5	242.9	247.4
GNP (i)	925.1	938.0	945.6	957.0	969.8	987.2	1003.1	1017.0	1031.5
(ii)	925.1	946.5	960.0	969.3	978.7	988.8	1000.2	1012.6	1026.2
(iii)	925.1	942.4	950.6	954.5	959.9	970.2	984.3	999.9	1016.3
(iv)	925.1	938.0	945.6	961.4	976.5	989.0	1000.3	1011.5	1025.0
GNP deflator (i)	1.272	1.289	1.306	1.318	1.329	1.338	1.349	1.357	1.364
(ii)	1.272	1.289	1.309	1.323	1.334	1.343	1.355	1.363	1.369
(iii)	1.272	1.289	1.307	1.320	1.330	1.338	1.349	1.357	1.363
(iv)	1.272	1.289	1.306	1.318	1.329	1.339	1.350	1.358	1.365
Corporate profits before tax (i)	87.2	85.7	83.4	82.6	82.6	84.8	87.1	88.8	91.0
(ii)	87.2	88.5	87.8	85.8	84.7	84.8	86.2	87.8	89.9
(iii)	87.2	87.6	85.8	82.7	81.0	81.3	83.1	85.2	87.8
(iv)	87.2	85.7	83.4	84.0	84.7	85.3	86.2	87.2	89.2
Unemployment rate (i)	3.47	3.71	4.08	4.24	4.10	3.97	3.85	4.00	3.97
(ii)	3.47	3.47	3.49	3.78	4.01	4.20	4.30	4.43	4.31
(iii)	3.47	3.73	4.05	4.59	4.96	5.06	4.96	4.85	4.58
(iv)	3.47	3.71	4.08	4.11	3.80	3.86	4.11	4.38	4.28

3. The Forecasts of August 1969.

During the last two weeks of July 1969, the preliminary estimates of *GNP* accounts and related economic data were assembled for the purposes of updating the data bank of the Wharton-EFU Model. New lag values were assembled, and new judgments were formed about exogenous variables.

A.I. Preliminary forecasts.

By August 1st, preliminary forecasts were available for four different alternative assumptions:

(i) The Administration's fiscal request—extension of the surcharge at 10 percent for the last six months of 1969 and at 5 percent for the first six months of 1970. Defense spending was assumed to decline gradually from the second-quarter values in real terms. Tight credit conditions were assumed to prevail until 1970.1. Farm income was assumed to peak in 1969.4 and the expansion of world trade was projected at a moderate pace, in comparison with faster growth in the past.

(ii) The fate of the tax surcharge was sufficiently in doubt that it seemed worthwhile to program a solution in which the whole surcharge was dropped (retroactively) from July 1, 1969. For this case, monetary policy was made stricter.

(iii) A variant of the dropping of the surcharge was a programmed solution in which federal government spending was reduced. The reduction started at $3.0 billion per quarter (annual rate) and expanded to a reduction of $8.0 billion per quarter. To compensate for the reduction in public expenditures, we made monetary policy slightly less strict than in (ii) but stricter than in (i).

(iv) The surcharge was assumed to be extended to December 31, 1969 and then dropped. The strict monetary conditions of (ii) were retained.

The results of the four preliminary tabulations are listed in Table A.I for selected variables of the model solutions.

A.II. Revised preliminary forecasts.

(i) The passage by the House of the Ways & Means Committee tax reform and tax relief bill, led to reconsideration of preliminary forecasts based on the provisions of taxing of capital gains and granting of higher exemptions for low-income classes. The abolition

110

of the investment tax credit (retroactive to April 1969) was already assumed in the first preliminary forecast calculations.

(ii) We did, however, make a second revised preliminary forecast in which additional effects were introduced to hold down investment as a result of the new treatment of depreciation in the tax reform legislation.

By the second week of August, we already knew the July report on personal income and could see that our projection for this variable was too low for 1969.3; we therefore raised some income variables in the solution to reflect what we already knew about personal income. Table A.II gives a summary of these two revised forecasts.

The revised preliminary forecasts were only slightly different from the original preliminary forecasts, as can be seen from a comparison of tables A.I and A.II. The expansive nature of lower tax rates implied for 1971 led to higher levels of economic activity generally in the last two quarters of the solution projection. These "far out" values are merely indicative, however, and not too much significance should be read into this difference.

A.III. Postrelease forecasts.

(i) As a result of our third-quarter meeting with business economists in the Wharton–Econometric Forecasting Unit, the basic input assumptions for Model solution were reviewed and slightly revised. Defense expenditures were reduced more than in the preliminary forecast solutions; civilian expenditures were increased more rapidly. These were somewhat offsetting. The government pay increase of July 1, 1969, was reapportioned, to be more concentrated in the seasonally adjusted figures for the third quarter, instead of being spread over the third and fourth quarters.

The tax revisions were rescaled and rearranged. They were assumed to be effective from 1969.4 instead of 1969.3; seasonally adjusted tax collections were assumed to reflect retroactive features in 1970.1 and 1970.2. Finally, the House bill was rescaled so that approximately only 70 percent of the originally announced provisions were assumed to appear in the final version.

Preliminary figures on the statistical discrepancy appeared to be larger than had been provided for in the original forecasts, and this adjustment had the effect of raising the corporate profits estimate. Also, preliminary figures become available for housing starts

111

Table A.II. Revised Preliminary Forecasts, August 8, 1969

		1969.2	1969.3	1969.4	1970.1	1970.2	1970.3	1970.4	1971.1	1971.2
Consumer expenditures	(i)	570.7	581.6	589.5	599.4	607.8	619.7	628.8	640.8	650.0
	(ii)	570.7	581.6	589.5	599.1	607.4	619.2	628.4	640.5	649.7
Fixed capital formation	(i)	98.5	99.6	98.4	96.3	95.9	94.9	94.8	94.4	95.9
	(ii)	98.5	99.6	98.4	95.4	94.8	93.8	94.8	93.2	94.8
Residential construction (nonfarm)	(i)	31.9	30.9	30.8	30.5	30.9	32.2	33.7	34.8	34.7
	(ii)	31.9	30.9	30.8	30.5	30.8	32.2	33.7	34.8	34.7
Inventory investment	(i)	9.5	7.9	4.3	2.6	2.1	2.4	3.5	5.0	6.4
	(ii)	9.5	7.9	4.3	2.4	1.9	2.2	3.4	5.0	6.4
Net exports	(i)	2.0	2.3	2.7	3.5	3.6	4.2	4.3	4.7	4.9
	(ii)	2.0	2.3	2.7	3.5	3.6	4.3	4.4	4.8	4.9
Government expenditures	(i)	212.5	217.3	222.2	226.1	230.1	234.2	238.5	242.9	247.4
	(ii)	212.5	217.3	222.2	226.1	230.1	234.2	238.5	242.9	247.4
GNP	(i)	925.1	939.6	947.9	958.3	970.3	987.6	1003.7	1022.7	1039.3
	(ii)	925.1	939.6	947.9	957.0	968.7	985.9	1002.2	1021.3	1037.9
GNP deflator	(i)	1.272	1.290	1.308	1.320	1.331	1.341	1.352	1.360	1.368
	(ii)	1.272	1.290	1.308	1.320	1.331	1.340	1.352	1.360	1.367
Corporate profits before tax	(i)	87.2	84.0	82.1	80.9	80.8	83.0	85.4	88.8	92.5
	(ii)	87.2	84.0	82.1	80.5	80.3	82.5	84.9	88.3	92.0
Unemployment rate	(i)	3.47	3.69	4.03	4.21	4.17	4.04	3.90	3.89	3.79
	(ii)	3.47	3.69	4.03	4.26	4.23	4.09	3.92	3.89	3.79

in July. These suggested that our residential construction equation was overestimating activity, and it was scaled down on the basis of the data at hand.

(ii) The main alternative to the control solution was one of higher defense spending coupled with retention of the surcharge indefinitely after January 1, 1970; i.e. the extension at 5 percent was assumed to be indefinite in duration instead of for six months only. The higher defense expenditures in this solution were symbolized by large ABM outlays. This provides for more hardware but not more military personnel.

(iii) A final solution variant was obtained in which the higher military outlays (advanced ABM systems) were associated with expiration of the surcharge after a six months extension at 5 percent for the period, January 1, 1970–June 30, 1970.

It should be pointed out that when the postrelease forecasts were made, preliminary estimates of second-quarter performance had been revised. The figure for corporate profits, which is one of the slower items to be reported, was made available from official sources for the first time. The postrelease calculations were therefore changed as a result of the discussion of the preliminary forecast results and assumptions, and new input assumptions were used for the August 18th calculations. In addition, new lag values became available. The result was not fundamentally different, but the *GNP* values were slightly higher in the later projections, and unemployment was correspondingly lower. The estimated *GNP* value for 1969.3 turned out to be just $2.1 billion under the preliminary estimate for that quarter, released in mid October. This was subsequently raised by $0.5 billion in November. The unemployment estimates were, however, too low in the postrelease calculations. They were quite correct for 1969.3 in the preliminary calculations.

A major implication of the August predictions, however, was a decline in real *GNP* in 1969.4, as a combination of relatively slow growth in current dollar *GNP* and rapid growth in the deflator. It is extremely difficult to pinpoint a *turn* in real economic activity, and this is the message that was coming from model projections in summer, 1969.

Each quarter's forecasting exercise involves a similar sequence of preliminary and revised forecasts, with several alternatives. If

113

Table A.III. Postrelease Forecasts, August 18, 1969

		1969.2	1969.3	1969.4	1970.1	1970.2	1970.3	1970.4	1971.1	1971.2
Consumer expenditures	(i)	572.8	582.3	591.1	601.8	610.4	622.3	631.8	643.5	653.1
	(ii)	572.8	582.3	591.5	602.7	611.5	620.0	628.5	639.7	649.0
	(iii)	572.8	582.3	591.5	602.7	611.5	623.6	632.8	644.4	653.8
Fixed capital formation	(i)	98.5	100.3	98.8	96.4	95.6	95.5	95.3	94.9	95.7
	(ii)	98.5	100.3	98.8	96.7	96.1	95.9	94.5	93.6	94.2
	(iii)	98.5	100.3	98.8	96.7	96.1	96.1	95.9	95.4	96.1
Residential construction (nonfarm)	(i)	32.2	30.0	31.1	30.8	30.9	32.2	33.9	34.9	34.4
	(ii)	32.2	30.0	31.1	30.9	31.0	31.9	33.4	34.5	34.2
	(iii)	32.2	30.0	31.1	30.9	31.0	32.2	33.8	34.7	34.2
Inventory investment	(i)	6.9	7.4	5.3	3.9	3.3	3.5	4.0	5.1	6.4
	(ii)	6.9	7.4	6.2	5.3	4.2	3.7	2.8	3.7	5.2
	(iii)	6.9	7.4	6.2	5.3	4.2	4.3	4.1	4.9	6.0
Net exports	(i)	1.6	2.3	2.7	3.4	3.1	4.2	4.3	4.7	4.4
	(ii)	1.6	2.3	2.6	3.3	3.0	4.2	4.3	4.8	4.5
	(iii)	1.6	2.3	2.6	3.3	3.0	4.1	4.2	4.6	4.3
Government expenditures	(i)	212.9	218.0	222.3	226.1	230.1	234.3	238.8	243.5	248.2
	(ii)	212.9	218.0	222.6	226.8	231.4	236.0	240.5	244.4	249.4
	(iii)	212.9	218.0	222.6	226.8	231.4	236.0	240.5	244.9	249.4
GNP	(i)	924.8	940.2	951.2	962.4	973.3	992.1	1008.1	1026.6	1042.2
	(ii)	924.8	940.2	952.9	965.7	977.2	991.8	1004.0	1021.2	1036.6
	(iii)	924.8	940.2	952.9	965.7	977.2	996.3	1011.2	1028.9	1043.8
GNP deflator	(i)	1.273	1.290	1.308	1.321	1.329	1.342	1.353	1.362	1.366
	(ii)	1.273	1.290	1.308	1.321	1.330	1.343	1.354	1.362	1.367
	(iii)	1.273	1.290	1.308	1.321	1.330	1.343	1.355	1.364	1.368
Corporate profits before tax	(i)	88.5	84.8	83.4	82.2	80.3	84.7	86.8	90.1	91.3
	(ii)	88.5	84.8	83.8	82.9	81.3	84.3	85.4	88.4	89.6
	(iii)	88.5	84.8	83.8	82.9	81.3	85.8	87.7	90.8	91.9
Unemployment rate	(i)	3.47	3.49	3.64	3.81	3.77	3.75	3.61	3.59	3.35
	(ii)	3.47	3.49	3.54	3.64	3.61	3.75	3.85	3.86	3.52
	(iii)	3.47	3.49	3.54	3.64	3.61	3.63	3.56	3.60	3.38

major events had occurred during late August, September, or early October, additional *flash* forecasts would have been generated. As things turned out, however, the next forecast rounds took place on approximately November 1, 1969, followed by a meeting to discuss results and assumptions, with new forecasts issued in mid November.

The results reported here are given in summary form, for convenience in presentation. The actual forecasts distributed, however, contained all the separate variables of the model and various interesting transformations or combinations of them.

B. SOME EXPERIMENTAL RESULTS
ON THE IMPROVEMENT OF PREDICTION[2]

In large samples with correctly specified models, the Mann-Wald and Haavelmo results would lead us to the estimation of dynamic systems by the method of full-information- maximum-likelihood, treating lag values of dependent variables as though they were like other predetermined variables (see p. 56 above). This procedure would provide optimal estimates of parameters and best predictions. In single-period predictions for small samples, it would seem best to treat lag values as wholly predetermined, but it is not clear that *FIML* estimation methods should be used, for they are known to be optimal only in the asymptotic case; however, there is little evidence to suggest that they would perform poorly in small samples if the model is correctly specified. Given the uncertainty of specification, though, it may be prudent and economical to use single-equation estimation methods such as two-stage-least-squares.

The issue, then, for realistic situations of prediction is to find best parameter estimates for multiperiod prediction in the small sample case. If complete systems of equations are to be used, this problem should be studied in the context of single-equation methods of estimation in order to minimize the possible effects of specification error.

[2]Messrs. Koji Shinjo and H.N. Johnston, fellows of the Wharton Econometric Forecasting Unit, have rendered invaluable assistance in the preparation of materials for this section.

115

Two types of experimental calculations will be described and analyzed here. (1) Sampling experiments with constructed data and assumed models will be discussed for the estimation and extrapolation of simple autoregressive schemes. (2) Actual data will be used to demonstrate the potential gains in predictive efficiency to be obtained by using iterated *TSLS* or *TSPC* methods (pp. 66–71) for estimation and extrapolation of the Wharton–EFU Model.

1. Sampling experiments

The simple autoregressive scheme
$$y_t = \alpha y_{t-1} + e_t$$
may be estimated over sample length $t = 1, 2, \ldots, T$ by the criteria

$$\sum_{t=1}^{T} (y_t - \alpha y_{t-1})^2 = \min \quad \text{OLS}$$

or

$$\sum_{t=1}^{T} (y_t - \alpha^t y_0)^2 = \min \quad \text{SEARCH}$$

The *SEARCH* method, so-called because of the computer technique used to find the optimal estimate of α, can be modified by minimizing

$$\sum_{j=1}^{F} \sum_{t=1}^{T} (y_{t+j} - \alpha^j y_t)^2.$$

In this version the generated lag values are for $F < T$ periods ahead. In the standard version, lag values are generated for the whole sample period of T units.

In the sampling experiments, random variables are drawn from the unit normal distribution and scaled to have a preassigned variance. The errors are serially independent. Specifications for a sample include

116

y_0 = starting value of y-series

L = total number of random drawings per replication after discarding p observations

p = number of observations discarded after y_o

σ = standard deviation of error

n = sample size for parameter estimation

m = length of prediction period

R = number of replications

α = population parameter.

For a given α and y_0, the selection of errors provides a series of y-values from

$$y_1 = \alpha y_0 + e_1$$
$$y_2 = \alpha y_1 + e_2$$
$$y_3 = \alpha y_2 + e_3, \text{ etc.}$$

Four different α levels are chosen over the interval $(0,1)$

$$\alpha = \begin{cases} 0.856 \\ 0.614 \\ 0.397 \\ 0.153 \end{cases}$$

Table B.I. Sum of Squares of Prediction Error: Autoregressive Process

Experimental specification	α	OLS estimate	SEARCH estimate	True α
y_0 = 200				
L = 80	0.856	406,202	453,265	404,196
p = 20	0.614	241,072	254,250	242,040
σ = 6				
n = 50	0.397	199,774	202,389	209,329
m = 10	0.153	183,396	183,927	182,743
R = 20				
y_0 = 200	0.856	57,715	57,678	51,696
L = 30	0.614	35,928	35,645	33,836
p = 20				
σ = 6	0.397	28,099	26,625	27,142
n = 20	0.153	24,292	23,908	23,915
m = 5				
R = 20				

After the first p observations are discarded, the next n observations are used for estimation of α (by *OLS* or by *SEARCH*). With the estimated value of α, predictions are made up to length m from $n + 1$, from $n + 2$, and so on, until the remaining observations are exhausted. The sum of squared prediction error is then recorded for each method and for the "true" parameter value. The experiment is then replicated R times.

A tabular presentation of the results of repeated sampling experiments are given in Table B.I.

In most cases, but not all, the true value of α provided better forecasts of length 10 and 5 than did the estimated values of α. For experimental samples of size 50, *OLS* outperforms *SEARCH;* for experimental samples of size 20 *SEARCH* is consistently better.

Two important experimental characteristics need to be varied —the initial value (y_o) and the size of the error variance (σ). By varying σ, we change the goodness of fit of the estimated relationship to the "observed" sample.

The initial values were made larger and smaller than $y_0 = 200$ for $\alpha = 0.614$ and 0.395. The results of this variant are in Table B.II.

Within these experiments, if the first twenty observations are discarded, the effects of the initial values (at either 400 or 50) are insignificant as far as forecast error is concerned. Also, within these experiments, *SEARCH* is better for small samples and *OLS* for large $(n = 50)$. This result confirms the findings in Table B.I. We conclude that the findings are not dependent on the particular initial values assumed. The basic patterns remain the same for

$y_0 = 400$

$y_0 = 200$

$y_0 = 50$

The residual variance was increased from 6 to 10 in these experimental calculations, and the basic patterns were unaffected.

The size of the variance was further varied for samples of size 50, but the superiority of *OLS* over *SEARCH* was unchanged.

The prediction results in the simplest model depend entirely on the estimation of one parameter, α. The method that makes the best estimate of α, also makes the lowest estimate of prediction

118

error. A richer model is one that includes an exogenous as well as a lagged variable:

$$y_t = \alpha\, y_{t-1} + \beta x_t + e_t.$$

In this model, x_t is realistically chosen from statistics on real government expenditures in the United States This series has a strong trend, and two variants were considered—with and without trend in x_t.

Table B.II. Sum of Squares of Prediction Error
(varying initial condition)

Experimental specification	α	OLS estimate	SEARCH estimate
$y_0 = 400$			
$L = 80$	0.614	669,645	706,250
$p = 20$			
$\sigma = 10$	0.395	554,931	562,193
$n = 50$			
$m = 10$			
$R = 20$			
$y_0 = 50$			
$L = 80$			
$p = 20$			
$\sigma = 10$	0.614	669,644	706,250
$n = 50$			
$m = 10$	0.395	554,931	562,193
$R = 20$			
$y_0 = 400$			
$L = 30$			
$p = 20$			
$\sigma = 10$	0.614	99,799	99,013
$n = 20$			
$m = 5$	0.395	78,053	73,958
$R = 20$			
$v_0 = 50$			
$L = 30$			
$p = 20$			
$\sigma = 10$	0.614	99,801	99,013
$n = 20$			
$m = 5$	0.395	78,053	73,958
$R = 20$			

Table B.III.   Sum of Squares of Prediction Error
(varying error variance)

Experimental specification	α	OLS estimate	SEARCH estimate
$y_0 = 200$			
$L = 80$			
$p = 20$			
$\sigma = 2$	0.614	26,786	28,250
$n = 50$			
$m = 10$	0.395	22,630	22,715
$R = 20$			
$y_0 = 200$			
$L = 80$			
$p = 20$			
$\sigma = 6$	0.614	241,072	254,250
$n = 50$			
$m = 10$	0.395	203,672	204,439
$R = 20$			
$y_0 = 200$			
$L = 80$			
$p = 20$			
$\sigma = 10$	0.614	669,644	706,250
$n = 50$			
$m = 10$	0.395	554,931	562,193
$R = 20$			
$y_0 = 200$			
$L = 80$	0.614	1,506,697	1,589,060
$p = 20$			
$\sigma = 15$	0.395	1,248,597	1,264,933
$n = 50$			
$m = 10$			
$R = 20$			

In the cases where x_t had a trend component, *OLS* performed better, and in the cases where x_t was trend-free, *SEARCH* performed better. In all cases, the "true" coefficients produced better predictions than either of the two estimates. The *OLS* estimates of α were smaller and those of β larger than in the *SEARCH* case. This meant that more weight was attached to the growing exogenous variable for the prediction period and naturally led to better forecasts for the *OLS* than for the *SEARCH* method of estimation.

The sampling experiments are still inconclusive. They do show, however, a negative finding, namely that *OLS* methods, while attractive, do not always lead to better predictions in dynamic models. It is not possible to generalize from the present experiments; they have not yet covered a sufficiently wide range of alternative specifications. Nevertheless, some interesting tentative observations are the following: (i) the larger the sample the smaller is the prediction error of *OLS* estimates of autoregressive schemes in comparison with *SEARCH* estimates. The latter minimize squared error along the simulation path. For small samples (20 or fewer in the present context), *SEARCH* methods of parameter estimation appear to lead to better forecasts than do *OLS* methods.

(ii) In mixed schemes with lags and exogenous variables, *SEARCH* methods do better than *OLS* if the exogenous variables used do not have trends.

(iii) *OLS* is a difficult method to beat in single-equation estimation. There are some instances in which other methods that do not regard lagged dependent variables as predetermined for estimation purposes perform better than *OLS* in prediction, but a general rule for improving upon *OLS* methods in the single-equation system has not yet been found.

2. Experiments with observed samples.

Another approach to experimental calculation is to use actual sample data in different ways and study some overall performance characteristics in trial applications. In particular, I shall examine the method of iterating two-stage-least-squares estimates, described on pages 66–71, for its contribution to the improvement of predictive power of a system.

The equation system to be examined is the Wharton–EFU Model.[3] This Model has been estimated by the *TSPC* method—two-stage-least-squares, using principal components of predetermined variables. In the first instance, one-period predictions over the sample span are compared for—

121

Table B.IV. Sum of Squares of Prediction Error—Mixed Autoregressive Process

Experimental specification	Exogenous variable	α, β	OLS estimate	SEARCH estimate	True α, β
$y_0 = 200$					
$L = 68$	with trend	$\alpha = 0.614$	681,879	693,185	590,697
$p = 20$		$\beta = 0.560$			
$\sigma = 6$	without trend	$\alpha = 0.614$	638,380	624,515	590,695
$n = 40$		$\beta = 0.560$			
$m = 10$					
$R = 50$					
$y_0 = 200$					
$L = 30$	with trend	$\alpha = 0.614$	102,436	107,254	84,615
$p = 20$		$\beta = 0.560$			
$\sigma = 6$	without trend	$\alpha = 0.614$	86,789	85,217	84,615
$n = 20$		$\beta = 0.560$			
$m = 5$					
$R = 50$					

(a) the Model as originally estimated by *TSPC*

(b) the Model estimated by regression of one dependent variable in each equation on $\hat{y}_{it}$ and x_{jt} in that equation. The variables $\hat{y}_{it}$ are obtained from the solutions of the system in (a). The process is not repeated after one iteration.

In a large system it would be remarkable if each method of estimation provided estimates of all coefficients that could be accepted on the basis of a priori information, such as signs, orders of magnitude, and statistical significance. In obtaining new estimates of the entire Model by iterating the *TSPC* estimates some equations are poorly estimated and throw the solution of the whole system far off the track. The offending equations are the production functions. Three different variants of the iterated *TSPC* estimates are therefore considered:

(i)   The parameters of the manufacturing production function are restricted to provide constant returns to scale.

(ii) The original *TSPC* estimated production functions (manufacturing and nonmanufacturing) are kept intact and used with the iterated *TSPC* estimates of the other equations.

(iii) The regression equation for manufacturing production is renormalized with log $h_m N_m$ as the *regressand*, together with an assumption that this production function shows constant returns to scale.

The question will not be whether some particular method of estimation, strictly followed, will produce a better forecasting system; it is whether there exists some set of estimates that can be readily found, and that produce a better forecasting system—both within and beyond the sample. The answer is in the affirmative; such a set of estimates can be found. They are very nearly iterated *TSPC* estimates, but not purely from this class. It does appear that iterated *TSPC* modified to permit variants (i), (ii), or (iii) are superior systems for purposes of prediction.

Although many individual variables or combinations of variables could be tabulated for simulation error, the seventeen variables

[3]See M.K. Evans and L.R. Klein, *The Wharton Econometric Forecasting Model* (Philadelphia: Wharton School of Finance and Commerce, University of Pennsylvania, 1968).

123

Table B.V. Root-Mean-Squared Error, Alternative Estimates of Wharton–EFU Model
One-Period Simulations, 1948.3–1964.4

	TSPC	(i)	(ii)	(iii)
Short term interest rate	0.211	0.210	0.210	0.210
Long term interest rate	0.112	0.111	0.111	0.111
Nonresidential investment (bill 1958 dollars)	1.724	1.582	1.582	1.582
GNP deflator (1958: 1.00)	0.005	0.004	0.003	0.003
Unfilled orders (bill 1958 dollars)	2.881	2.482	2.492	2.492
Residential investment (bill 1958 dollars)	1.055	1.071	1.072	1.072
Personal income (bill current dollars)	5.460	4.685	3.643	3.512
Corporate profits (bill current dollars)	4.124	4.510	3.888	3.905
GNP (bill current dollars)	7.338	4.670	4.412	4.398
GNP (bill 1958 dollars)	7.343	4.721	4.518	4.557
Unemployment rate (percent)	1.564	1.713	1.312	1.392
Consumer expenditures (bill 1958 dollars)	5.006	3.856	3.497	3.581
Inventory investment (bill 1958 dollars)	3.442	2.207	2.204	2.207
Net foreign balance (bill 1958 dollars)	1.384	1.542	1.590	1.618
Employment (millions)	1.049	1.331	0.958	1.035
Index of working week (40 hours = 1.0)	0.009	0.004	0.004	0.004
Earnings (thous. current dollars)	0.048	0.046	0.044	0.045

TSPC refers to the original estimates of the Wharton–EFU Model.

(i) Refers to iterated TSPC estimates, with manufacturing production at constant returns to scale.

(ii) Refers to iterated TSPC estimates except for production functions, which are the original TSPC estimates (manufacturing and nonmanufacturing).

(iii) Refers to iterated TSPC estimates with the manufacturing production function renormalized and restricted to have constant returns to scale.

124

listed are representative of all aspects of the model and the economy. These are the standard variables used for analysis in the meeting on cyclical content of econometric models held by the Conference on Research in Income and Wealth.

An examination of the entries in Table B.V, shows that root-mean-squared errors ($RMSE$) are significantly lower for some of the more important variables when $TSPC$ estimates are iterated. The production functions are poorly estimated by a mechanical application of the iteration method; this is apparent on looking at the individual parameter estimates and shows up strongly in simulation of the whole model. The iterated versions (ii) with original production function estimates and (iii), with renormalized and constrained production function estimates, seem to offer the best estimates when measured by one-period simulation performance. Version (ii) is better in most cases, but version (iii) is close to (ii) in $RMSE$ magnitudes. In only two cases does the original system show minimal $RMSE$. Since the equations for interest rates are purely recursive, the performance measures for these variables are the same for all methods in one-period simulations. The differences recorded in Table B.V are purely the result of rounding or minor data revisions. Some of the data used now for the iterated schemes have been slightly revised, and it was not possible to make a precise reconstruction of all the series actually used for the $TSPC$ estimates made in 1966. The same is true for nonresidential investment, but the discrepancies are a bit larger. Rounding to one decimal, however, the comparisons are between $RMSE$ of 1.7 for $TSPC$ and 1.6 for (i), (ii), or (iii).

In the cases where $TSPC$ performs best, the superiority of its $RMSE$ measure is not large. The comparisons, however, for central variables like GNP and personal income are striking and not a consequence of data revision. Reduction of $RMSE$ from amounts in excess of 7 to amounts less than 4.5 are of extreme significance. $RMSE$ of 5 is typical of many econometric models and a good standard of reference. The iteration methods appear to improve on this standard. In the case of personal income, the reduction from approximately 5.5 to 3.5 is equally significant. Reduction of $RMSE$ for other variables in Table B.V are possibly less dramatic but nevertheless important.

Although the application of the extra-step iteration procedure

125

Table B.VI. Root-Mean-Squared Error, Alternative Estimates of Wharton–EFU Model
One-Period Extrapolations, 1965.1–1968.4

	TSPC	(i)	(ii)	(iii)
Short term interest rate	0.512	0.517	0.517	0.517
Long term interest rate	0.212	0.213	0.213	0.213
Nonresidential investment (bill 1958 dollars)	2.812	3.988	3.988	3.988
GNP deflator (1938: 1.00)	0.005	0.003	0.002	0.002
Unfilled orders (bill 1958 dollars)	6.279	2.667	2.671	2.610
Residential investment (bill 1958 dollars)	1.552	1.616	1.619	1.589
Personal income (bill current dollars)	36.163	36.958	35.830	28.060
Corporate profits (bill current dollars)	8.972	9.194	8.608	5.216
GNP (bill current dollars)	22.926	25.009	24.231	18.852
GNP (bill 1958 dollars)	17.694	20.794	20.418	15.924
Unemployment rate (percent)	0.982	1.415	1.349	0.745
Consumer expenditures (bill 1958 dollars)	12.870	18.949	18.566	14.065
Inventory investment (bill 1958 dollars)	8.993	3.171	3.143	3.114
Net foreign balance (bill 1958 dollars)	6.253	3.502	3.417	3.148
Employment (millions)	2.141	3.255	3.196	1.825
Index of working week (40 hours = 1.0)	0.016	0.006	0.006	0.007
Earnings (thous. current dollars)	0.683	0.688	0.689	0.691

is not quite as explained as pages 67–68, because of the difficulty in getting satisfactory production function estimates, it is clear in the present application that there exist plausible estimates of *structural* parameters that improve within-sample simulation performance. If the criterion for goodness of a whole model is minimization of *RMSE* for simulation, we can find better estimates than those commonly used, although we cannot claim to have found estimates that minimize *RMSE* for particular variables.

Similar results have been found for the Wharton–EFU Model by George Treyz.[4] In his study, Treyz iterated the *TSPC* estimates by using as regressors *selected, important* components of *GNP* estimated from the solution of the complete Wharton–EFU System (*TSPC* form) in *selected important* equations of the Model. A mixed system was simulated consisting of the iterated estimates for nine selected equations and *TSPC* estimates for all the other equations. This method is called regression-on-predicted (*ROP*) estimation by Treyz. As in Table B.V above, he finds improvement of prediction error for the whole system over the sample period by using *ROP* estimates for some equations. In ex-post forecasts beyond the sample, he also finds superior results from the *ROP* system.

A reason for the improvement of simulation performance of the Model when iterated *TSPC* estimates are used is that this technique reduces the amount of simultaneity in the system and relies more heavily on predetermined variables—either lagged or exogenous for one-period simulations. The regression coefficients for the effect of computed regressands on the normalized dependent variables tend to fall in absolute value because the computed regressands in the iterated method have smaller variability than do the corresponding regressands in the ordinary application of *TSPC* method. In the simulations, there is more reliance on the observed predetermined variables and less on the simultaneous variables. This tends to lower *RMSE*.

A stringent test for superiority of iterated *TSPC* methods is comparison of their performance against that of *TSPC* estimates in extrapolation beyond the sample period. These are one-period

---

[4]These results are reported in the joint paper by M.K. Evans, Y. Haitovsky, and G. Treyz (see notes to the Original Edition, p. 46, note 1).

Table B.VII. Root-Mean-Squared Error, Alternative Estimates of Wharton–EFU Model Two-Period Extrapolations, 1948.1–1964.4

	TSPC	(i)	(ii)	(iii)
Short term interest rate	0.212	0.213	0.213	0.213
Long term interest rate	0.157	0.160	0.160	0.160
Nonresidential investment (bill, 1958 dollars)	2.105	1.895	2.196	2.385
GNP deflator (1958: 1.00)	0.007	0.006	0.006	0.006
Unfilled orders (bill 1958 dollars)	4.159	4.089	4.074	4.093
Residential investment (bill 1958 dollars)	1.053	1.031	1.040	1.034
Personal income (bill current dollars)	6.313	5.283	4.178	4.460
Corporate profits (bill current dollars)	4.540	4.703	4.255	4.676
GNP (bill current dollars)	9.171	6.260	6.321	6.861
GNP (bill 1958 dollars)	8.796	5.751	5.967	6.552
Unemployment rate (percent)	1.605	1.912	1.284	1.699
Consumer expenditures (bill 1958 dollars)	5.442	4.184	3.859	4.280
Inventory investment (bill 1958 dollars)	3.490	2.571	2.651	2.757
Net foreign balance (bill 1958 dollars)	1.600	1.946	2.098	2.180
Employment (millions)	1.183	1.567	0.977	1.289
Index of working week (40 hours = 1.0)	0.007	0.005	0.005	0.005
Earnings (thous. current dollars)	0.059	0.058	0.055	0.058

ex-post forecasts. In Treyz' study, he found that the new estimation method gave better results in extrapolation. The results for complete reestimation of the Wharton–EFU Model are in Table B.VI.

In this case method (iii), which performs all right but not quite as well as (ii) within the sample period, outperforms all methods in ex-post extrapolations beyond the sample. These results are partly due to the renormalization and partly due to the one-round iteration of *TSPC* studied here.

The errors in Table B.VI are clearly large, either in absolute value, considering the magnitudes involved, or in comparison with the sample period solutions. It is, of course, expected that the errors will rise during an extrapolation period, but one might ask whether they have risen too much. Mechanical ex-post forecasts generally tend to have larger errors than we tolerate in practice. Ex-ante forecasting by the methods outlined above are much more accurate because they involve the use of a priori information together with the statistically estimated system. This practice reduces error considerably; nevertheless, even with large error, the results in Table B.VI indicate suggestive relative rankings of methods.

A further extension of iterated *TSPC* methods is to the case of dynamic simulation and multiperiod prediction. It will require substantial analysis to consider all the possible comparisons of *path*, rather than *point* prediction and also to consider variation in the prediction horizon; therefore only the simplest extension is treated here—to two-point prediction. In this case, one-period lag values are developed as computed values in sample period system solutions for estimation purposes, and these replace observed lag values, as they are used as in the standard procedures.

In the sample period, there is unqualified improvement in using iterated *TSLS* estimates, extended to the dynamic case, over the original Wharton Model coefficients.

Although the three alternatives are not always uniform among themselves, they are each generally better than the original *TSPC* estimates for purposes of two-point prediction. The main aggregates, in particular, are better estimated by the iteration methods with the dynamic extension.

A more difficult test of the dynamic iteration method is in extrapolation beyond the sample to 1965.1–1968.1. Method (iii) is outstanding, as in the one-period prediction tests, but its superiority

129

Table B.VIII. Root-Mean-Squared Error, Alternative Estimates of Wharton–EFU Model
Two-period Extrapolations, 1965.1–1968.1

	TSPC	(i)	(ii)	(iii)
Short term interest rate	0.512	0.544	0.544	0.544
Long term interest rate	0.352	0.357	0.357	0.357
Nonresidential investment (bill 1958 dollars)	6.223	6.865	6.258	5.024
GNP deflator (1958: 1.00)	0.015	0.008	0.007	0.005
Unfilled orders (bill 1958 dollars)	5.781	3.863	3.855	3.826
Residential investment (bill 1958 dollars)	1.590	1.706	1.694	1.655
Personal income (bill current dollars)	34.206	44.268	40.588	31.300
Corporate profits (bill current dollars)	6.803	5.073	4.441	4.661
GNP (bill current dollars)	25.201	40.245	35.970	26.580
GNP (bill 1958 dollars)	15.174	30.877	28.200	21.018
Unemployment rate (percent)	1.919	2.610	1.940	0.838
Consumer expenditure (bill 1958 dollars)	9.479	20.594	19.084	14.115
Inventory investment (bill 1958 dollars)	7.700	7.377	6.670	5.513
Net foreign balance (bill 1958 dollars)	7.623	3.888	3.616	3.131
Employment (millions)	2.252	4.365	3.813	2.093
Index of working week (40 hrs. = 1.0)	0.009	0.007	0.007	0.007
Earnings (thous. current dollars)	0.679	0.689	0.688	0.689

is marred by the fact that it does not perform better with respect to some important variables like GNP and consumer expenditures. In the post-sample extrapolations, there is generally a bias in projecting consumer expenditures by all methods, but this bias appears to be greater for the iterated than for the ordinary $TSPC$ estimates. In actual forecasting, it is usually possible to detect bias after some initial mistakes; therefore, this kind of error is not necessarily indicative of the weakness of a method or model. In spite of the poor showing for GNP, the method used in column (iii) of Table B.VIII does provide improvement over standard $TSPC$ estimates for ten of the seventeen variables tabulated.

The major categories for which the iterated $TSPC$ results appear to be better in two-period forecasts (column iii) are strongly fluctuating and residual-type variables. These are nonresidential investment, unfilled orders, corporate profits, unemployment rate, inventory investment, and net foreign balance. These are all unusually difficult to predict and significantly causal in economic fluctuations. Were it not for the bias in estimating consumer expenditures, the iterated methods may have performed better in estimating the main aggregates, too.

The iterated estimates of parameters in individual equations were accepted regardless of magnitude or sign, with the exception of the manufacturing production function, where we renormalized and restricted returns to scale. In practice, we would not blindly accept just any parameter estimates that happened to come out of the calculation procedure. We would want to impose some a priori restrictions on size and sign of the estimates. If we adjust the iterated estimates by deleting variables where coefficients change sign and then make extrapolations, there is a slight improvement in the size of the root-mean-square errors. The GNP and consumption prediction errors are reduced by about $1.0 billion. Most other predictions are also improved. This improvement in GNP predictions is not large enough, however, to bring the errors down to the level of those generated by the ordinary $TSPC$ method.

An overall accuracy measure that summarizes results on several variables simultaneously is average absolute percentage error. This particular measure is sensitive for residual or balance variables that can be negative, zero, or positive and have small mean values. Inventory change and net foreign balance are typical examples.

131

Although profit and unemployment are also residual variables, they are more strongly positive and less troublesome in terms of percentage accuracy for all methods used. The iterated *TSPC* estimates, either for one- or two-period extrapolations perform much better than the ordinary *TSPC* estimates for inventory change and net foreign balance; therefore, tabulations of average absolute percentage error that delete these two variables from the average are favorable to the ordinary *TSPC* method; yet the iterated methods have superior scores for this statistic, as shown in Table B.IX.

These are two-point *path* estimates of error; i.e. the errors for a given model are taken from both one-period and two-period extrapolations. The iterated estimates are from the same model that was used for column (iii) of tables B.VII and B.VIII; they use generated lags of one period as well as generated values of unlagged dependent variables. In forecasts beyond the sample period, the iterated method shows the strongest degree of superiority over the ordinary *TSPC* estimates, and the relative score would be much more impressive if the two deleted variables were to be included.

The experiments to date are suggestive of the possibility of improving prediction accuracy. Any gains are to be valued highly since the goal of accurate prediction is commonly accepted as one of the primary objectives of economic science; yet these potential gains must be placed in proper perspective.

It appears that percentage errors can be reduced by approximately one point or that *GNP* errors might be cut by $1–3 billion

Table B.IX. . Average Absolute Percentage Error*

Within Sample:	One-period extrapolation	Two-period extrapolation
Ordinary TSPC	4.36	4.83
Method (iii), two-period dynamic estimates	4.33	4.57
Beyond Sample:		
Ordinary TSPC	5.73	6.29
Method (iii), two-period dynamic estimates	4.75	5.33

*Errors for inventory investment and net foreign balance omitted.

132

if parameter estimates are improved towards meeting a prediction objective. While these potential gains are significant they are much smaller than the gains that might be realized if models are better specified, if data are made more accurate and plentiful, if more and better a priori information are used in both specification and prediction. Eventually, these bigger gains might reduce prediction error by a factor of one-half, while the gains from better methods of estimation should, at the outside, reduce prediction error by 20 percent and more likely by approximately 10 percent.

INDEX

ABM outlays, assumptions about in forecasts, 113. *See also* Defense spending
A priori information, use of in prediction, 51, 55, 96, 100, 105, 107, 129, 133.
    See also Expert information
Adams, F.G., 45–47, 90
Adelman, I. and Adelman, F.L., 97–99, 104
Adjustments of constants, in prediction, 50–51, 106–7
Aggregation, 78ff.
Aitken estimator, 61
Algorithm: for solutions of nonlinear systems, 23; for minimization of
    prediction error, 64
Analog computation, 65
Anticipatory variables: endogenous generation of, 88; use of in forecasting,
    87–88
Attitudes, 87
Autoregressive errors, 52–55, 107. *See also* Serial correlation
Autoregressive model, 43, 94–96, 100, 102, 116ff.
Autoregressive structure, 16–18
Average absolute error, 39–40; percentage, 131–32

Backcasting, 13
Bronfenbrenner, M., 13
Brookings Model, 23, 78; sector analysis, 81–85, 89
Brown, T.M., 29
Burns, A.F., 90

Cassel, G, 18
Characteristic equation, 17, 63
Cochrane, D., 53, 62
Cohen, K.J., 65
Coinciding series, 91–93
Commerce, Model of U.S. Department of, 47, 104. *See also* OBE Model
Complete solution, 17
Consistency, 57, 61
Control solution, 77, 111–113
Cooper, R.L., 66
Crow, R., 104
Cycles, 18
Cycles, Analysis of by National Bureau of Economic Research, 90–93,
    96, 99
Cycles, simulation of, 97–98
Cycles, spectral analysis of, 98–99, 104

Maximum likelihood, method of, 33, 65, 72–74, 115
Microeconomic data, 87
Mitchell, W.C., 90
Moore, G.H., 90, 93
Moving average process, 19
Multicollinearity, 67
Multiplier, 18, 75ff.; dynamic, 76, 77; impact, 75, 76; Keynesian type, 75; nonlinear, 76–77; static, 77
Multi-stage least squares, 66ff.

Nagar, A.L., 24, 29, 34, 35, 42–43, 46, 51, 80, 94, 96
Naive model, 42–43, 46, 51, 80, 94, 96
National Bureau of Economic Research, 46; indicator methods of, 90–93, 96
Neyman, J., 27
Newton-Raphson method, 71
Noise, 27
Nonlinear model, 22, 35
Nonlinear multiplier, 76–77
Normalized dependent variable, 68

OBE Model, 47, 104. *See also* Commerce, Model of U.S. Department of
OBE–SEC investment intentions, 87
Objective methods of forecasting, 9, 48
Odeh, H.S., 29, 34, 35
Orcutt, G.H., 17, 53, 62, 95

Particular solution, 17
Political predictions, 11
Popkin, J., 47
Population projections, 11
Predetermined variables, 67, 127. *See also* Exogenous variables and Independent variables
Prediction, bias in, 40–41; conditional, 13, 21, 93, 101, 103; defined, 10; deterministic, 15; ex ante, 13, 19, 20, 21, 28, 38, 41–42, 46–47, 93, 129; ex post, 13, 20, 28, 34, 38, 41–42, 47, 71–73, 81, 85–86, 88, 127, 129; industry, 85–86; judgment in, 48; mechanistic, 42, 48, 129; microeconomic, 82; multi-period, 19, 55–56, 129ff.; single-period, 18, 19, 27–29, 55–56; social, 10; stochastic, 15, 20, 21, 26; unconditional, 13
Prediction, variance-covariance error of, 65
Presidential elections, prediction of, 11. *See also* Electoral prediction
Principal components, 67, 71–74, 79, 116, 121–26
Psuedo sample, 36, 37

Rational function lag distribution, 18
Realization equations, 86–87
Reduced form, 15, 16, 18, 22, 24, 25, 28–32, 51, 75, 96, 100; restricted, 68